More Words I Love to Recite

More Words I Love to Recite

An Earthly/Heavenly Dialogue

CHARLES SANTIAGO

RESOURCE *Publications* • Eugene, Oregon

MORE WORDS I LOVE TO RECITE
An Earthly/Heavenly Dialogue

Copyright © 2025 Charles Santiago. All rights reserved. Except for brief quotations in critical publications or reviews, no part of this book may be reproduced in any manner without prior written permission from the publisher. Write: Permissions, Wipf and Stock Publishers, 199 W. 8th Ave., Suite 3, Eugene, OR 97401.

Resource Publications
An Imprint of Wipf and Stock Publishers
199 W. 8th Ave., Suite 3
Eugene, OR 97401

www.wipfandstock.com

PAPERBACK ISBN: 979-8-3852-6772-9
HARDCOVER ISBN: 979-8-3852-6773-6
EBOOK ISBN: 979-8-3852-6774-3

These love poems are dedicated to
Soul mates in and out of
Space and time.

Contents

Introduction | *xvii*
1. Heaven's Fragrance | 1
2. Newfound Life | 2
3. Grief | 3
4. We Declare | 4
5. Two Homes | 5
6. Our Demand | 6
7. Because of You | 7
8. "Alive and Here" | 8
9. Steady, Steady | 9
10. Patient, Be! | 10
11. Eternity, Won! | 11
12. Heaven's Not So Far Away | 12
13. Believe Me, | 13
14. Be Yourself | 14
15. My Lady | 15
16. Heaven Is | 16
17. *Just* Your Clay | 17
18. A Heavenly Palace | 18
19. Overcome with Glee! | 19
20. Every Day of Every Year | 20
21. Remember Wedding Number Three | 21
22. A Higher Way | 22
23. Surprised by Love | 23
24. *One, We Are* | 24

25. Watching Movies | 25
26. You and I | 26
27. Heaven's Not Beyond Your Reach | 27
28. *Heaven's* Sun | 28
29. Heaven's Sway | 29
30. How Deep Our Love Can Be! | 30
31. Our Love | 31
32. I Can Tell | 32
33. Inspired by Heaven's Glow | 33
34. Singing in the Key of C | 34
35. Live Our Life! | 35
36. Our Earthly Time | 36
37. Communion | 37
38. A Happy Séance | 38
39. Till My Final Day | 40
40. Death Has Lifted You and Me | 41
41. We Are Seekers | 42
42. No Mere Accident | 43
43. Heaven's Glow | 44
44. In Every Way, a Unity | 46
45. More and More | 47
46. You're Not Gone | 48
47. Embrace Me, Dear | 49
48. Reason to Crow | 50
49. Heaven's Light | 51
50. Oh, the Joys We Share! | 52
51. A Perfect Ending to a Perfect Day | 53
52. Kanapaha Joy | 54
53. Lovely Gardens, Shining Bright | 55
54. This Path We've Trod | 56
55. A Monster You Must Slay | 57
56. We Are Free | 58
57. Heaven's Lovely Glow | 59

58. What a Gift! | 60
59. I'm Content | 61
60. Let Us Rejoice | 62
61. Oh, the Joy That Death Can Bring! | 63
62. No Greater Thrill | 64
63. Not Alone | 65
64. Our Past | 66
65. No Need to Wait | 67
66. I Have Come | 68
67. I Am Trusting You Will Be | 69
68. Join Me on the Other Side | 70
69. Sharing Heaven's Glow | 71
70. A Garden | 72
71. A Better Place | 73
72. What Better Place? | 74
73. Heavenly Ties | 75
74. Our Mighty, Peaceful Bond | 76
75. More than Memories | 77
76. O Great Resurrection Day! | 78
77. Oh, What Joy a Garden Brings! | 79
78. Imagine | 80
79. Beyond What Words Can Tell | 81
80. Light from Heaven | 82
81. More than Clay | 83
82. We Found Eternity! | 84
83. A Higher Life | 85
84. Oh, the Joy, to Be, *as ONE!* | 86
85. Your Faith | 87
86. I Feel You Near | 88
87. Three Weddings | 89
88. My Creed | 90
89. Remember to Recite Our Creed | 91
90. Eternal Union | 92

91. A Ladybug and Bumblebee | 93
92. A Door | 94
93. This Union | 95
94. You Haven't *Died* nor Have You *Left* | 96
95. Love Will See Us Through | 97
96. We Are *One*, It's True! | 98
97. Our Heavenly Mirth! | 99
98. Be Wise! | 100
99. Oh, How Sweet, This Bond of Ours! | 101
100. A Letter from Heaven | 102
101. God Is Love | 103
102. Come Fly with Me! | 104
103. You Are Learning | 105
104. A Happy Bumblebee | 106
105. Matters of the Heart | 107
106. Wedding Bells | 108
107. Our Niche | 109
108. It's, *as If* | 110
109. Eventide, 1 | 111
110. Eventide, 2 | 112
111. Eventide, 3 | 113
112. A Special Day | 114
113. Heaven's Spring | 115
114. Angels | 116
115. Rhyme with Me | 117
116. To *Resurrection*, I Am Wise | 118
117. Our Lovers' Lane | 120
118. What a Brute I'd Be! | 121
119. Soul Mates | 123
120. The Love We Share | 125
121. A Diploma | 126
122. Means, at Hand | 127
123. Death Is Dead! | 128

124. We'll Bill and Coo | 129
125. The Spring | 130
126. I'm Not Gone! | 131
127. A Palace of Light | 132
128. Do Not Doubt | 133
129. It's You! | 135
130. This Lovely Home | 136
131. A Morning Talk | 137
132. A Friend of Mine | 138
133. Walk with Me in Timbuktu | 139
134. A Pact | 140
135. Our Union Didn't End | 141
136. One Home | 142
137. Thirty Earthly Years | 143
138. All My Life | 144
139. You *Know* Me, Dear | 145
140. Let's Explore | 146
141. Recall the Love We Shared, Below | 147
142. By and By | 148
143. Rejoice with Me! | 149
144. Rejoice and Sing, My Earthly Beau! | 150
145. What a Life! | 151
146. True Lovers | 152
147. Love Is Stronger than the Grave | 153
148. I'm Not Entombed | 154
149. By Your Side | 155
150. Remind Yourself | 156
151. A Lovely Couple | 157
152. To Live, *as One*, Despite My Clay | 158
153. Heaven Bound | 159
154. Rescued from the Mortal Sting! | 160
155. God Has Joined Us! | 161
156. Moldering Bodies | 162

157. Sad and Lonely Nights | 163
158. Always, Dear, a Unity | 164
159. This Strange and Wondrous Life | 165
160. Death, at Last, Was Not Our Foe | 166
161. You're a Temple | 167
162. If, Today, My Voice, You Hear | 168
163. Joy for Me | 169
164. Remember | 170
165. Woo and Coo | 171
166. Heaven's Lovely Dance | 172
167. I Believe | 173
168. When We Married | 174
169. You Haven't Left! | 175
170. Don't Be in a Hurry! | 176
171. Two Worlds | 177
172. Here—and There | 178
173. To the Grave | 179
174. The Open Door | 180
175. Heaven | 181
176. Heaven's Joys | 182
177. A Holy Union | 183
178. When I Reach My Last Earth Day | 184
179. In Praise of Unity | 185
180. By Your Faith | 186
181. This Special Rendezvous | 187
182. A Higher Form | 188
183. A Better Way | 189
184. Quite a Mystery | 190
185. A Sad, Sad Tale | 191
186. Dance with Me! | 192
187. Dancing | 193
188. In Your Body, I Abide | 194
189. Just a Note | 195

190. Study *Well* Your ABCs! | 196

191. Always Near! | 197

192. In Greater Sunshine, Now, We Bask! | 198

193. Happy Birthday, Bumblebee! | 199

194. From Your Side, I Didn't Go! | 200

195. Eternal Joy | 201

196. This Heavenly Glow | 202

197. I *Do* Declare! | 203

198. My Life, Below, in Timbuktu | 204

199. Tuesday, at Two | 205

200. We'll Reminisce | 206

201. When Our Days on Earth Are Through | 207

202. *Apart*, My Dear, We Cannot Be! | 209

203. A Heavenly Life | 210

204. Peace, Joy, and Love | 211

205. Anniversary Poem from Earth | 212

206. Anniversary Dialogue | 213

207. When the Earth and Sun Are Gone | 214

208. Glory in Our Newfound Love! | 215

209. Always | 217

210. Your Life of Light | 218

211. Heavenly Wings | 219

212. Life Beyond the Grave | 220

213. There and Here | 221

214. A Heavenly Birth | 222

215. Where I Live | 223

216. I Am You, and You Are Me | 224

217. Sweethearts for Eternity | 225

218. Sweet Communion | 226

219. Our Continued Union | 227

220. Eve and Adam | 228

221. Anniversary, 1 | 229

222. Anniversary, 2 | 230

223. Anniversary, 3 | 231
224. Angels, Guiding | 232
225. Eternal Life, as Man and Wife | 233
226. Melding | 234
227. Joined, in Death, We're Joined, in Life | 235
228. Angels, Helping | 236
229. Our Life, *as One* | 237
230. The Memory of Our Life on Earth | 238
231. Let a Billion Years Go By! | 239
232. I'm Resolved | 240
233. Words That Ring So True! | 241
234. When the Time Is Right | 242
235. I'm a Spirit | 244
236. This Body | 245
237. All Your Days | 246
238. A *Couple*, We Can Be | 247
239. Evidence of Our Communion | 248
240. Angels Help Us | 250
241. I Dwell Within Your Heart | 251
242. Rendezvous! | 252
243. A Bridge | 253
244. When a Man Becomes a Beau | 254
245. Love's Great Power | 255
246. Rhyming | 256
247. Night and Day | 257
248. Our Lovely Creed | 259
249. A Double Bliss | 260
250. More than We Know | 261
251. Time Can't Sever You from Me | 262
252. When Bodies Die | 263
253. Within | 264
254. Think, Each Day | 265
255. Heavenly Treasure | 266

256. I'm Still Me! | 267
257. A Love, Divine | 268
258. Despite My Clay | 269
259. Despite Your Clay | 270
260. God Delights in You and Me, | 271
261. We Have Found, Dear, What We Crave | 272
262. Our Life Is Not Through! | 273
263. I'm a Happy Man! | 274
264. My Goal | 275
265. Completely Done! | 276
266. Our Life on Earth, | 277
267. Let's Rehearse | 278
268. Mighty Angels | 279
269. Heavenly Breezes | 281
270. The Quiet Roar of Eternity | 282
271. You and I Were Raised! | 283
272. Our Happy Unity | 284
273. Nighttime Is the Time to Fly | 285
274. This Heavenly Rest | 286
275. You And Me! | 288
276. Our Heavenly Rendezvous | 289
277. Eternal Love | 290
278. I See No Need to Grieve | 291
279. Forty-Nine Months | 292
280. Recite These Words | 293

Introduction

> *Darling, you're my one true love—*
> *THERE, below, and HERE, above.*
> *In and out of time and space,*
> *We are joined in love's embrace.*
>   (181. "This Special Rendezvous," verses 1–4)

WHEN MY WIFE DIED and passed into the afterlife, I followed her into the afterlife and became a different man living in some kind of different time zone. My wife and I were married for 30 years. Poem 181, "This Special Rendezvous," partially quoted above, was written four years after my wife's passing. I am writing *these* words, two years and two months after that poem was written. For six years and two months, my wife and I have been living "in and out of time and space." These six years and two months have been the most remarkable period of my life. The experience catapulted me into the realm of poetry, as I tried to make sense of this life-changing event.

Before my wife's passing, she had pointed out to me on several occasions that we were soul mates. Looking back, our 30 years together seem to have zipped by in no time. On the other hand, the six years since her passing seem like 60 years! I often wish that our time together in time and space had been longer. I think, though, that, by heaven's design, we had *just* the right amount of earthly time together that we needed. As I have come to see, it's *not* like our time together had *ended* when she died. The poems declare that the event of my wife's "passing away" was actually a second wedding for us. Furthermore, the event of *my* "passing away" will be a third wedding for us, a wedding beyond the realm of night and day. Between weddings number two and number three, we live "in and out of time and space." It's like, somehow, living in two different worlds simultaneously. The first four verses of poem 171, "Two Worlds," state:

> *Two worlds*, I know, my heav'nly belle—
> *One*, real *well;* one, **not** so *well*.
> Every day, I face the two,
> Searching, dear, for only *you!*

    I discovered the second world because my wife was correct when she had told me that we were soul mates. We had never discussed the topic. She had merely pointed her observation out to me. Before she died, we didn't have any kind of discussion about reaching out to each other if one of us died before the other. What I discovered, though, was a constant stream of bizarre occurrences and uncanny coincidences in my daily life that would make complete sense if they were viewed as instances of my wife trying to catch my attention and to communicate with me! She couldn't *do* so, physically, because her physical body was gone. But she *could* do so, through bizarre situations that I found myself in, that would cause me to reflect and wonder if maybe she was reaching out to me from the afterlife. I have found that heaven can communicate to me through how the events of my daily life unfold. In the beginning, I would write down accounts of these bizarre occurrences and uncanny coincidences so that I wouldn't forget them, but they began to happen so frequently that I gave up on trying to maintain a written record of them. I have recounted a few of these occurrences and coincidences in some of the introductions to my previous books.

    Beyond these signs from heaven as a means of communication between us, though, is the spiritual reality of our awareness of each other. In the writing of our poems, I don't actually *hear* the words of my wife that I write down as coming from her. Communicating *with words* ("the ABCs," "the alphabet," or "A through Z," in the poems), whether spoken or written, is something below the level of heavenly communication. But, since I am still *here*, the working out of communication between us, *in words*, is a concession *to me*—and, by extension, to those who read the poems.

    The poems are love letters between soul mates, an earthly beau and his heavenly belle. Our love is stronger than the grave and, so, we've found the love we crave! The first and last stanzas of Poem 119, "Soul Mates," read as follows:

> "Soul mates" were the words you used,
> Describing how our souls were fused.
> "Thou, beside," you said, to me,
> Before I was a bumblebee. . . .

> Dear, this creed has brought me life.
> It proves that we're still man and wife.
> "Soul mates"—*yes,* my heav'nly belle—
> Way back then, you knew it *well!*

    I hope that, as people read these poems, they would consider that, loved ones who have died are not "dead and gone." They are "alive and here" if we will sharpen our senses to feel beyond the physical realm. We are spiritual beings living in physical bodies. Our union with a loved one does not have to be presumed to be ended at death, for love *never* dies.

Poems

1. Heaven's Fragrance

Charles Santiago, 4/28/23

Heaven and Earth are not apart!
I know it, deep within my heart.
You have, dear, admonished me—
"A married couple, still, are we."

No joy on Earth can match this love.
With *you*, I meet, dear, *there*, above.
And, yet, I'm clothed with Earthly clay
And count the hours, night and day.

Yes, it's *you!* I know it's *so.*
I've *learned* to recognize your glow.
Heavens! Darling, I'm amazed.
These Earthly eyes are heaven–glazed.

God be praised, my heav'nly belle!
Heaven's fragrance, I can smell.
We have *trounced* Man's ancient foe
And left our sorrows, all, below.

2. Newfound Life, 4/29/23

Celebrate with me, each day,
This newfound life, my Earthly beau.
We have found a higher way
Beyond the reach of Man's great foe.

Angels help both you and me
To live this newfound life, my dear.
They are helping us to be
Familiar with our home, UP HERE.

Man and wife, dear, we remain.
OF COURSE, it's SO, my bumblebee!
Death resides BELOW our plane.
He CAN'T destroy our unity.

***I** am **grateful** you believe*
In newfound life for me and you.
As you learn, dear, not to grieve,
GREATER, is our rendezvous.

3. Grief, 4/29/23

Grief, my dear, is unbelief.
BELIEVE—and lose your woeful grief!
Grief will close the heav'nly door.
Grief is SUCH a frightful bore.

Grief is spawned by human brawn.
MIGHTY Man wails "DEAD AND GONE!"
Oh—that Man could ONLY learn
HOW, that Earthly life, to spurn!

The MORE you learn, dear, to BELIEVE,
The LESS, my darling, you will grieve.
The LESS, grief has his hold on you,
The GREATER, dear, our rendezvous.

HIGHER, darling, do we rise,
The MORE that frightful idler dies.
Believe in God. Believe in me,
And grief can't help but set you free!

4. We Declare, 4/30/23

I declare, my heav'nly belle,
You've released me from my cell.
I am free to meet with you
Beyond the bounds of Timbuktu.

I declare, my bumblebee,
God has freed us, you and me,
To sail upon a heav'nly sea
And, from your prison, to be free.

Let us sail, then, on this sea,
You and I, in ecstasy.
I'm so happy to be free,
Sailing on this sea with thee!

Angels, darling, help us glide
On this sea on heaven's side.
I am thrilled to be your bride
AS we, IN God's love, abide!

5. Two Homes

Charles Santiago, 4/30/23

Now begins another day,
Walking in this heav'nly way.
My days, enslaved to time, are through
Because I'm married, dear, to you.

All the days, this Earth, I roam,
I'm conscious that it's not my home.
My home is *there*, my love, with you,
Beyond this Earth with sky, so blue.

Blue, myself, I couldn't be,
For, dear, you dwell inside of me.
As we've *said*, two homes, have we—
Inside of me, and *there*, with thee.

The Earth, itself, could never be
A home, my dear, for you and me.
It was just a start, you see,
For living in eternity.

6. Our Demand

Charles Santiago, 4/30/23

A sunbathing poem

Kiss me on the lips, my love.
How I yearn for heav'nly bliss!
From our love nest, *up above,*
Thrill me with a tender kiss!

Darling, I'm in love with you
Beyond what I can understand.
Two hearts, bound as *one*—not *two*—
Life, beyond the grave, demand.

Like the glory of the sun,
Shines this love that owns us, dear.
Eve and Adam, still, are *one*.
Love can never disappear.

Our demand is small, my love,
In view of our Creator's might.
God, who flung the stars above,
Saves us from our Earthly plight.

7. Because of You

Charles Santiago, 4/30/23

A sunset poem

The more I shut the world away,
The deeper, dear, this rendezvous.
Dear, I don't know *what* to say,
Except for *this*—Our love proved true.

Precious is this life we share.
Death has proved to be a dud.
How I love to prove a dare
And *find* I'm *more* than flesh and blood!

I'm a part of heaven, above!
Every day, I find it's *so*.
It's because of *you,* my love.
You have *claimed* your Earthly beau.

Before you "left," my heav'nly belle,
Sunset was your great delight.
And, **now**, my darling, *I* can **tell**,
Sunset, *still,* suits *you* just *right*.

8. "Alive and Here," 5/1/23

When that monster, DEAD AND GONE,
Tries to slay you, bumblebee,
Don't fight back with Earthly brawn—
Just remember YOU AND ME.

YOU AND ME will see you through,
EVERY TIME, my Earthly beau.
DEAD AND GONE cannot undo
Unions fused by heaven's glow.

Let us write a brand-new song.
"Alive and Here," we'll name it, dear.
It will help you get along
When, its lovely strains, you hear:

> *Alive and here, alive and here—*
> I can feel you EVER near,
> Singing sweetly in my ear:
> "Soul to soul, we now adhere."
>
> *Alive and here, alive and here—*
> Sounding certain, loud, and clear.
> When, its sweet refrain, I hear,
> DEAD AND GONE must disappear.
>
> *Alive and here, alive and here—*
> Like a mighty, gleaming spear—
> Protects the truth I hold so dear
> And slays, completely, mortal fear.

"Alive and Here," my darling Charles—
Sing it when that monster snarls.
I'm alive, and **I** am here.
Dear, I'll never disappear!

9. Steady, Steady, 5/1/23

Greenwise Market
Tallahassee, Florida

We needed no more time on Earth
To garner, dear, this heav'nly mirth.
The past and present blend, as one,
WITHOUT or WITH that Earthly sun.

Deeper is our love, today,
Than WHEN we WALKED that Earthly way.
Do not grieve the past, my love.
Concentrate on life, ABOVE.
If you DO, then you will see
HOW much, DEAR, our lives agree.

Steady as she goes, my beau,
THERE where deathly breezes blow.
WE can NAVIGATE this sea—
Concentrate on YOU AND ME.
YOU AND ME is what we are,
Shining like a heav'nly star.
I'm so proud of you, my dear,
Finding life we share, UP HERE!

This heav'nly mirth we've found, my love,
Is ours, forever, HERE ABOVE.
Steady, steady, bumblebee—
Concentrate on YOU AND ME.

10. Patient, Be! 5/1/23

A sunbathing poem

I'm not gone, dear. I'm not gone!
Do not be, of death, a pawn!
Don't believe those Earthly eyes.
A human spirit never dies.
I'm alive, and I AM HERE.
Share with me, dear, heav'nly cheer.
DEAD AND GONE, dear, must depart
From your mind and from your heart.
Yes, it's hard to understand.
Dear, I offer you my hand.

Clasp my hand and rise with me
Above that murky, Earthly sea.
WE are doing WELL, my love.
HOW we FIT like hand in glove!
PATIENT, be, dear bumblebee!
Life's not ALWAYS ecstasy.
Take delight in ME AND YOU,
Strolling through this rendezvous.
PLEASANT, will our journey be,
Living in eternity!

11. Eternity, Won! 5/1/23

A sunset poem

*More than you **know**, my Earthly **beau**,*
*Wherever you **go**, I LOVE you **so**;*
*For, YOU are, to **me**, my ecsta**sy**—*
*My reason to **be**, dear bumble**bee**!*

*WE were made **one**, below Earth's **sun**.*
*Now, HEAVEN, we've **won**, while YOU'RE on the **run**.*
*I'LL be with **you**, in all that you **do**.*
*To YOU, I'll be **true** till sunsets are **through**.*

*THEN we will **fly** beyond Earth's blue **sky**.*
*THEN you and **I** will NEVERMORE **sigh**;*
*For, WE will be **done** with Earth's lovely **sun**.*
*Eternity, **won**, we'll NO LONGER **run**.*

12. Heaven's Not So Far Away, 5/2/23

Do you seek me, bumblebee?
Close your eyes, and you will see,
Heaven's not so far away,
If you'll only trust and pray.

Trust and pray, my Earthly beau,
AND, with ME, to HEAVEN, you'll GO.
Die to unbelief and see
YOU'RE in HEAVEN, here, with me.

You can feel me feeling you—
That's because our life's not through.
THROUGH, my love? You and me?
THROUGH, my love, we'll NEVER be!

We have found a special place,
In and out of time and space.
If you trust and pray, each day,
Easier*, you'll find the way.*

Do not fear the body's end.
Heaven's just around that bend.
Live, each day, above Earth fears,
And YOU'LL be SPARED those Earthly tears.

Sing our song, "Alive and Here."
JOYFUL, be, each day, my dear.
*I **am** "**alive** and **here**" with **you**.*
Enjoy, my love, our rendezvous!

13. Believe Me, 5/2/23

Believe me, darling, when I say,
*I **walk** with **you**, each Earthly day.*
Believe me, when I say to you,
*I **love** you **there**, in Timbuktu.*

IF you ONLY would BELIEVE,
YOU would NEVER, EVER, grieve!
I'm, STILL, your love, my Earthly beau—
The one who WALKED with you, below.

Do not be, my bumblebee,
Like THOSE, below, who WILL not SEE.
WILL your way to me, above,
BY the POWER of our love!

Walk with me, in heaven, each day.
Angels, dear, will lead the way.
***I** am **so** in love with you,*
No one else, for me, will do!

14. Be Yourself, 5/2/23

Be yourself, my bumblebee.
***I** will **watch** with utter glee!*
***You're** the **one** I love to see.*
You ARE, my dear, the OTHER ME!

Bumble, to your heart's content.
YOU'RE my BEAU, from heaven, sent.
Dear, I've called you "bumblebee"
Because you work, SO HARD, to see—

To see this life God gives to us,
Aboard this resurrection bus!
*I chose **you**, my Earthly man*
Because I knew we'd live again!

Live again, each Earthly day,
With ME, in THIS, our heav'nly way!
Be yourself, and I will be
In love with you, my bumblebee!

15. My Lady

Charles Santiago, 5/2/23

Darling, let me say,
You *brighten* every day.
If *I'm* your *other me*,
It's *what* I *like* to *be*—
A busy, bumbling bee.

I'd *like* to *call* you "ladybug,"
But *then* I ponder and I shrug—
A *bug*, my dear, you *couldn't* be!
Heavens! What got into me?

A "lady," though, fits *to a tee*,
And *so*, "my *lady*," *you* will *be*.
"Worms" and "grubs"—and "bumblebee"—
Are terms more fitting *just* for *me*.

My lady—I will wait on thee.
A bumbling scribe is what I'll be.
With my pen, these rhymes, I'll write,
Until, one day, I *get* one *right!*

16. Heaven Is, 5/2/23

*Heaven is HERE, love. Heaven is **HERE**—*
*In your **HEART**, in your **HEAD**, in your **EYE**, and your **EAR**.*
Heaven is YOU, and heaven is, dear,
WHEREVER, on Earth, you FEEL that I'm NEAR.

Heaven is US and, always, will be
A LADYBUG TEASING her DEAR bumblebee.
Heaven is LOVE, dear, between you and me,
A gift, from our Maker, of pure ecstasy!

Heaven, my dear, is a HE and a SHE,
Praising their Maker, like you and like me.
Heaven is YOU, from your body, SET FREE,
Our beautiful home, in the heavens, to see.

17. *Just* Your Clay

Charles Santiago, 5/2/23

A sunbathing poem

Just your *clay*, you *lost*, my *dear,*
That *day* I **thought** you *left* from *here—*
Just your *clay,* a passing thing,
Like wrapping paper, bound by string.
What a ***fool*** was ***I,*** to think
That *clay* is *such* a vital link!
What a *waste—*those tears of mine—
As *if,* my love, you *weren't divine!*
Heaven help this blind man, love,
Unschooled in life from up above!

Having learned our brand-new song,
"Alive and Here," I can't go wrong.
"Alive and Here," I'll chant, each day,
As, hand in hand, we make our way.
Dead and Gone, I'll, *no more,* hear.
*Dead and Gone—*It's very clear,
Is *just* a lie that blind men hold,
As if, somehow, it brought them gold.
Loved ones, leaving clay, behind,
Aren't *dead,* or *sleeping, deaf,* or *blind.*
Dying loved ones leave their clay,
But, *really,* haven't *gone away.*

18. A Heavenly Palace

Charles Santiago, 5/2/23

A sunbathing poem

I close my eyes and think of you,
And, dear, you prove our love is true;
For, *you* remind me, in my soul,
That you and I are, still, one whole.
I am ***learning MORE***, each day,
Secrets of the heav'nly way.
Bodies are not needful, dear!
I can *feel* you *still*, down *here!*
How I love this life we share—
Yes, it's *just* because *we dare!*

Ladybug, my one true love,
I ***know*** just ***what*** I'm ***speaking of***.
For thirty years, down here, below,
Your precious soul, I came to know.
And, *now*—your loving, Earthly beau—
I *recognize* your heav'nly glow!
Of this *love*, I *stand* in *awe*—
We've, truly, found our Shangri–la!
A heav'nly palace, dear, is ours,
Beyond the ken of Earthly powers!

19. Overcome with Glee! 5/3/23

Heaven's all around you, dear,
Every day of every year.
Heaven waits for you to see,
From TIME and SPACE, dear, WE are FREE!
Don't be blind, and don't be numb.
Speak of love, dear. Don't be dumb!
FEEL and SEE—and SPEAK to me.
Be a HEAV'NLY bumblebee!

I am *learning* how to see,
Every day, you're next to me.
I am *learning* how to feel,
Dear, our joy is very real!
I'm *even* learning how to speak
From a lofty, heav'nly peak.
Anoint my eyes. Clasp my hand.
Speak to me of heaven's land!

Now, my dear, train your ear,
Music, from ABOVE, to hear.
How complete you, THEN, will be—
To HEAR, to SPEAK, to FEEL, and SEE.
Heaven's all around you, love.
Heaven's below, and heaven's above.
Every day you walk on Earth,
Join me, dear, in heav'nly mirth!

I am *overcome* with glee—
A *heav'nly* bumblebee, to be!
To *hear*, to *speak*, to *feel*, and *see*,
There, in heaven, dear, with thee,
Fulfills my every Earthly dream.
Things, below, aren't *as* they *seem*.
While I *live* on Earth, *below*,
Up above, with you, I grow!

20. Every Day of Every Year

Charles Santiago, 5/3/23

All the things, down here, I do
Are things, my dear, that *you* do, *too;*
For, *one,* we *are* and, *one,* we'll *be,*
Now, and for eternity.

Please, excuse my blindness, dear.
I've *lived,* myself, so *long,* down *here,*
That *it's* not *easy* to understand
How things *work* in heaven's land.

But *this* I'm learning—*You* can *see*
All, down here, that's done by me.
You're engaged in *this,* my life,
As *still* my loving, caring wife.

Take the blindness from my eyes!
Help me see beyond Earth skies!
Alive and *here,* are *you,* my dear,
Every day of every year.

21. Remember Wedding Number Three, 5/3/23

I am *waiting,* ladybug,
In my bed, all warm and snug.
Do you have a word for me
Before I bumble out, to be,
A busy, bumbling bee for thee,
To see if, *heaven,* I can see?

See, my bee, if you can be
So BUSY, as a bumblebee,
That YOU can LEARN, from A to Z,
HOW, from worry, to be free.
You and I can be our best
WHEN you GET things OFF your CHEST.

My biggest worry, my heav'nly bride,
Is fear of wand'ring from your side.
Since that woeful day you died,
I *feel,* sometimes, without a guide.
Darling, I am at my best
When *you* and *I* are home, at rest.

God is able, bumblebee,
To keep you, from that worry, FREE.
Weren't we, dear, made INTO ONE,
By wedding vows beneath Earth's sun?
Remember—Wedding number three
Will clinch this heav'nly ecstasy!

22. A Higher Way

Charles Santiago, 5/3/23

A sunbathing poem

All my love, to Thee, I give,
O God, who gave me life to live.
While I'm *garbed* in Earthly clay,
I will *seek* a higher way—
A higher way that calls to me
To walk, much closer, God, to Thee.

A babe, a lad, and now a man,
O God, I seek to live again.
When this body dies, O God,
Returning to the Earthly sod,
Give me raiment, shining bright,
That rescues me from day and night.

23. Surprised by Love, 5/3/23

Inspired by "Breaking of the Shells" by Billy McLaughlin

We are still entwined, my dear,
Though I'm living "way up here."
WE'RE not IN a bind, my love.
We've GOT this HOME, above,
That's BIG ENOUGH for me and you
While, below, we rendezvous.

Can you feel, my Earthly beau,
The wondrous power of our glow?
With a love so great as THIS,
*WE don't NEED an **EARTHLY** kiss.*
Hand in hand, let's EVER grow,
Loving God, who loves us SO!

Yes, my dear, two HOMES, have WE,
In which to share this ecstasy!
*Could we love LIKE THIS, **BEFORE**—*
Before we opened heaven's door?
No, my love, this love we share
Has got a special, heav'nly air!

24. *One, We Are*

Charles Santiago, 5/3/23

Were *I* the *only* man on Earth,
By my side, you'd make your berth.
You and I will always be,
By our choice, a unity.
It is God Almighty who
Joined us when we said "I do."
God, who made us, made us for
A life, *as one,* forevermore.

I *feel* you *more,* today, my dear,
Than *when* you had a body, here.
The spirit, far, exceeds the flesh,
In its power to enmesh.
Sealed, my darling bride, are we,
For life through all eternity.
We who walked the Earth, in clay,
Walk in heaven's eternal day.

One, we *are,* down here, below.
From my *side,* you didn't go.
One, we *are,* in heaven, "above,"
By virtue of eternal love.
You are *me,* and *I* am *you*—
Every day, we prove it's true.
Now, I'm turning out the light,
Bidding you, my dear, "Good night."

25. Watching Movies, 5/3/23

Dear, I've claimed you—as you know.
How I love to tell you SO!
YOU are claiming ME, my beau,
Every day you walk, below.
***I** am **yours**, and **you** are **mine**—*
Darling, this is love, divine!
Our thirty years, REMEMBER, love!
They're a movie, HERE, above.

Watching movies is a link
To ME, my dear, more THAN you THINK.
All those films you watch, my dear,
Are times, for us, of special cheer.
Clark Gable, dear, is who you are.
You're my favorite movie star!
Boy-meets-girl is always fresh.
Even NOW our souls enmesh!

Remember, please, my bumblebee—
I'm always ME. I'm always ME!
CLOSER, dear, we grow, each day.
I'm not drifting far away!
Greta Garbo and Myrna Loy,
Dear, they serve me, as a ploy.
By their charms, I pull you in—
In TO a date in Heaven's Inn.

26. You and I, 5/4/23

I have found you, bumblebee.
I have found you seeking me.
You have found we still agree.
You have found our unity.

You have found me seeking you.
You have found our love is true.
No matter what the world may do,
Darling, we are never through!

We'll continue, you and I.
We have found we do not die.
Neither you nor I need cry.
Lovers never say goodbye.

27. Heaven's Not Beyond Your Reach, 5/4/23

In your body and your soul,
We are ONE, dear. We're one WHOLE.
I am living, dear, IN YOU.
***ONE**, we ARE, and NEVER **TWO**!*

Don't you think, because you're CLAY,
WE can't SHARE in heaven's day.
Heaven's not beyond your reach—
Study what the angels teach.

WE don't HAVE to wait, to be,
Sharing heaven's ecstasy.
*I **repeat**, dear bumblebee,*
*I AM **YOU**, AND **YOU** ARE **ME**!*

28. *Heaven's* Sun

Charles Santiago, 5/4/23

When the daylight comes, my dear,
Heaven isn't *quite* as near.
Nighttime brings those special hours,
Alive with bright, angelic powers.
Shining stars, like Sol, my love,
Obscure the light from heaven, "above."
Heaven's sun, that shines so bright,
Makes *shining stars,* all, *sons* of *night.*

My! The things I've learned, my love,
Since we've *found* our home, above.
I'd *never* have believed it, dear,
That *you* could *be—quite* this near.
To truly know of heaven's worth,
Earthlings need a brand-new birth.
I was **shocked** into this life
When *you became* my *heav'nly* wife!

29. Heaven's Sway, 5/4/23

A sunbathing poem

Trust me, sweetheart, when I say,
We have found a higher way.
Believe your hunches, every day.
Thrill, with me, to heaven's sway!
THERE, on Earth, when skies are gray,
Heav'nly promptings, dear, obey.
Though you still are robed in clay,
You can leave Earth's disarray.
Like a Spaniard, shout "Olé!"
I'll appear, dear, come what may!

Come what may, I'll always know,
Though I'm still an *Earthly* beau,
I can feel your heav'nly glow.
I can tell, dear, we still grow.
Dear, it wasn't long ago,
You and I beat Adam's foe.
Now I, *up* to heaven, go,
Though I tread this Earth, below.
Life is heaven, dear, and—oh!
I adore you, head to toe!

30. How Deep Our Love Can Be!

Charles Santiago, 5/4/23

A sunset poem

With faith and love, I seek you, dear;
And, by those two, I find you *here*.
Oh, how blind, I sometimes am,
And find myself in such a jam!
Our love, my dear, endures.
You're *mine*, and I am *yours*;
But, *forward*, I must go,
And rise to heaven's glow.

Without this faith that feeds my love,
I'd never rise to thee, above.
My Earthly eyes deceive me, dear,
Proclaiming you're not really here.
Thank *God* for *faith* to *know*
You didn't, *up* and *go!*
Thank *God* for love, divine.
I *feel* that *you're* still *mine!*

All the while I live, below,
I'm conscious of your heav'nly glow.
A *living pair*, my love, are we,
Joined in *such* an ecstasy!
I'm eager, dear, to see
How *deep* our love can be,
That day God *calls* me *home*,
On Earth, no more, to roam.

31. Our Love

Charles Santiago, 5/5/23

Our love, my dear, is freeing me—
Freeing me from gravity.
I'm giddy as a boy who's found
A toy that lifts him off the ground.

Our love has kept our hearts *as one*
While, yet, I'm trapped beneath the sun.
I feel a warm and tingling glow
That doesn't come from *here,* below.

Our love has saved me from a fear
That reigns supreme on Earth, down here—
I haven't *lost* you, dear.
You *didn't* disappear!

Our love has changed me, inside out.
We've conquered death—I *have* no *doubt*.
I'm living *now*, with *you*.
My life, on Earth, is through.

32. I Can Tell

Charles Santiago, 5/6/23

Like a man raised from the dead,
I am free from every dread.
As if I had been born *again*,
I *feel* like an *eternal* man!
I can feel a strange, new light
From a land devoid of night.
Though, their forms, I cannot see,
Friends, I feel—in love with me.
Dear, it's all because of *you*,
Alive with me in Timbuktu.

I can tell, my heav'nly belle,
This is *you*! I *know* you *well*.
From our home in heaven, "above,"
You delight to share your love.
You have claimed me, dear, I know.
I am yours, your Earthly beau.
Heavens, dear! I'm all in awe.
How *divine*—this Shangri-la!
Dear, from Earth, I'm claiming you
Till these Earthly days are through.

33. Inspired by Heaven's Glow, 5/6/23

Live your life, dear, there below,
All inspired by heaven's glow.
As, about your work, you go,
We continue, dear, to grow.
Do not think it strange, my love,
We OWN a MANSION, here above.
What was meant for me and you,
That lovely day we said, "I do,"
Was THIS—a life, for you and me,
Filled with heav'nly ecstasy.

You have claimed me, bumblebee,
*Like **I** have **claimed** you, **just** for **me**.*
We've a life to live, my love,
That's filled with glory, here above.
*"**You** are **me**, and **I** am **you**"*
Let's chant until your days are through.
Love, my dear, has found us out,
Freeing us from fears and doubt.
Live your life, my Earthly beau,
All inspired by heaven's glow.

34. Singing in the Key of C

Charles Santiago, 5/6/23

A sunbathing poem

I *know* you, dear. I *know* you, dear!
I *know* you didn't disappear!
I *attest* that *you're* still *here*—
Not only, *here*, but *very near.*

As I live this life, below,
I can tell, we, *onward,* go.
Here, where deathly breezes blow,
Communion, sweetheart, *still,* we know.

More fulfilled, I couldn't be.
There's no *sweeter* harmony—
Singing in the key of C,
Crooning songs of *You and Me.*

To God, our Maker, dear, we owe
Vict'ry over Adam's foe.
Sweetheart, *how* I *love* you *so*—
Signed, your bumbling, Earthly beau.

35. Live Our Life! 5/7/23

Live our life, my Earthly beau,
HERE, above, and THERE, below.
Trust in God—and angels, too.
Trust, my dear, in ME AND YOU.

Remember, dear, our thirty years
With gratitude—and shed no tears.
WHAT a GIFT they were, my love,
Shining STILL up here, above.

Walk with me, dear, hand in hand.
We are MEANT for heaven's land.
Oh, BELIEVE, in all you do,
YOU can FIND me seeking YOU!

I am walking, dear, with you.
*It's the thing I **love** to do!*
Live our life, my bumblebee.
God will grant you eyes to see!

36. Our Earthly Time, 5/7/23

Darling, all our Earthly time
Is—HERE, in heaven—MORE sublime.
Do not think you LOST me, dear.
Death, to you, has brought me near.
HOLD on, dear, with ALL your might,
To FAITH AND LOVE—a shining light.
I could never forget our love,
Especially, in our home, above.
Holy angels will SEE us THROUGH
The Earthly things that YOU must DO.

YOU keep thinking that we're APART
When, more than ever, we SHARE one HEART!
I am THERE, right next to you—
Believe, each day, that it is true!
*I am **happy**, my darling Charles,*
NEXT TO YOU, through Earthly snarls.
Let your body rant and rave,
All the way, dear, to the grave.
Bodies rant and rave, my dear,
Until it's time to come UP HERE.

37. Communion, 5/7/23

A sunbathing poem

Yes, it's true, my Earthly beau—
You and I, **communion**, *know.*
Of course, it's SO, my bumblebee.
You and I could never be
APART, my dear, as YOU or ME.
I'm SO GLAD, this truth, you see;
For, darling, you're the one I love—
Signed, your sweetheart, here above.

Truth be told, I *know* it's *so;*
And, yet, my dear, it's *hard* to *know.*
Every day, I do my best
To join you, in our heav'nly nest.
Life, for me, is only *this—*
To share, with you, our wedded bliss.
No joy on Earth compares, my dear,
To union *still*, with you, down here!

38. A Happy Séance, 5/7/23

In the spirit, let's unite
At the outset of this night.
I can feel a heav'nly glow.
Heaven now is reaching low.
I'm prepared, the truth, to hear—
The truth that says that *you* are *here*.

You are *here*. I *know* it's *so*.
We continue, dear, to grow.
Though it seem, to me, quite strange,
I pray you speak within my range.
I recall our Earthly love—
A gift, to us, from God above.

Likewise, dear, let's *now* commune.
Like they say, down here, let's "spoon."
Joyful union is our due.
You are *me,* and *I* am *you*.
Greater, let our joy now be
Than *merely Earthly* ecstasy.

Why should we not share, dear wife,
Still, a happy, holy life?
I'm prepared to grow some wings,
In place of Earthly wedding rings.
You reach low, and *I'll* reach high,
And let us, through the heavens, fly!

I proclaim my love for you.
Ever, dear, I vow, "I do."
You are all my happiness,
In this *Earthly* wilderness.
God has joined us, dear, *as one,*
For *more* than *just* an Earthly run.

My one and only love, are YOU!
To our vows, dear, I am true.
Death, to you, has brought me near.
I rejoice IN YOU, my dear!
ONE, my Earthly beau, are we—
Eternally, a He and She.

God *gives* ***you****, dear,* ***faith*** *and* ***love****,*
So *to rise to heaven, above.*
In the spirit, we unite—
JUST like ON this LOVELY NIGHT.
CLOSER, is our union, dear.
IT'S still ME, dear. Don't you fear!

"She is GONE and FAR AWAY"—
SO, the world, will always say!
Recall our Earthly love and KNOW—
Just like THEN, we STILL can grow.
Heaven's not a barren land!
We can still walk, hand in hand!

In the spirit, dear, be brave.
Do not listen to the grave.
Believe your hunches, bumblebee,
And SEE how CLOSE you ARE to ME.
Why would I be LESS, my love,
Because I now live HERE, "above?"

Tonight, we've had a lovely time.
Our union, dear, is SO sublime!
A happy séance, we have had,
To keep you, dear, from being sad.
If you ONLY knew, my dear,
HOW our love is GREATER, here!

39. Till My Final Day, 5/8/23

Greenwise Market
Tallahassee, Florida

Of course, my dear, you'll always be
Walking *here*, each day, with me.
There's no need for me to fear,
My dear, you'll *up* and disappear!
Till my final day on Earth,
Our love will show its sterling worth.
I'm so thankful for this life
Of Earthly man and heav'nly wife!
Death, my dear, is not our foe.
On our *merry way*, we go!
I'm a fool to doubt it's *so*—
Even as I feel us grow!

Feel us grow, my Earthly beau.
The MORE you DO, the MORE you'll KNOW,
THERE'S no way I'll disappear!
I'm the OTHER YOU, my dear.
Throw your doubts and fears away.
Your heav'nly hunches, dear, obey.
BELIEVE ME, darling, COME WHAT MAY,
I am with you EVERY DAY!
Faith and love work, hand in hand,
To transfer you to heaven's land.
Darling, we have all we need.
Every day, recite our creed.

40. Death Has Lifted You and Me, 5/8/23

Heaven is HERE. Heaven is HERE!
YOU don't HAVE to DIE, my dear!
WE have ALL we need, my love,
THERE, below, and HERE, above.
Can you feel our love expand
While you tread that Earthly land?
Take it easy, there below.
Rejoice with me, my Earthly beau!
THERE'S no need, FOR DEATH, to pine.
Heaven NOW is yours and mine.
We've SUFFERED NO DEFEAT.
Our love is still complete!

We will always be like THIS—
Sharing heaven's lovely bliss.
Our THIRTY YEARS, on EARTH,
BEGAN this HEAV'NLY MIRTH.
Know, for sure, in all you do,
There below, in Timbuktu,
I am stuck to you like glue;
*For, **I am**, **dear**, THE OTHER YOU.*
Death has lifted you and me,
To share this heav'nly ecstasy!

41. We Are Seekers

Charles Santiago, 5/9/23

When your body died, my love,
When you "left" for heaven, "above,"
You and I remained, *as one.*
Our life, together, wasn't done.

Distant, you are *not,* my dear.
I can *feel* you *still,* down here.
Together, we still spend each day—
But *in* a *higher, heav'nly* way.

When I seek you, *you* I find!
I can see, dear. I'm not blind!
But *this,* my dear, I also see—
You are busy seeking *me!*

We are seekers, you and I.
I've discovered death's big lie.
"Dead and gone," he cries, each day,
While we *seek* and *find* our way.

42. No Mere Accident, 5/9/23

Inspired by the film *Stamboul Quest*,
1934 starring Myrna Loy and George Brent

Myrna Loy, you *are*, to *me*—
Just as *sweet* as you can be!
How I love to feel you, dear,
In the films I watch, down here!
Somehow, dear, you feel *so real*,
In these films, from reel to reel.
"*Watching movies is a link
To ME, my dear, more THAN you THINK.*"
Yes, it's true, my heav'nly bride—
We watch *movies*, side by side.
You, in Myrna Loy, appear.
Art is part of heaven's sphere.

*George Brent, my Earthly beau, are YOU.
Through his art, we bill and coo.
Romantic love, my bumblebee,
FOREVER'S true for you and me.
That "veil" we used to talk about,
Is RIPPED in TWO; for, THERE'S no DOUBT—
MOVIE STARS, are YOU and I,
Reciting lines, dear, eye to eye.
Through the magic of the spheres,
Earth time simply disappears.
You and I, and Loy and Brent,
Meet, by no mere accident.*

43. Heaven's Glow, 5/10/23

I believe, yes, I **believe**;
Therefore, dear, I **will** not **grieve**.
I believe that you're alive.
I believe that we still thrive.
I believe in you and me,
From the sting of death, set free!
"Union" means, for me and you,
Death must bid us, now, adieu.
One, we are, and *one,* we'll be,
Now and through eternity.

Heaven calls us both, my dear,
TO this HOME we have, up here.
I AM YOU, AND YOU ARE ME,
Guarantees our liberty.
Grieve, no more, my bumblebee.
Walk, with me, in heav'nly glee.
We are destined for this life
As Earthly groom and heav'nly wife.
Leave, behind, the fears of Earth.
Walk, with me, in heaven's mirth.

I am learning, more and more,
How to enter heaven's door.
You are helping me to see
Heav'nly life for *you and me.*
Wedding bells, I hear, my love,
Calling me to life, above.
I will say goodbye to Earth,
Guided by our heav'nly mirth.
Why should I consent to walk
In a land where we can't talk?

WE'RE enjoying, you and I,
Pleasures of the by-and-by.
Death was just our entranceway
To heaven's brighter, joyous day.
I'm alive within you, dear.
You're alive with me, up here.
As your life unfolds, below,
A higher life, above, we know.
You BELIEVE, my Earthly beau,
And, SO, we walk in heaven's glow!

44. In Every Way, a Unity

Charles Santiago, 5/10/23

I *feel* you *in my body*, dear!
I admit, it's mighty queer;
But I am thrilled that we can be,
In every way, a unity!

One, we are, my heav'nly belle—
Even in my Earthly shell.
I am you, and you are me—
To be *so one* is ecstasy!

Let this Earth explode, my love—
Still, we have our home above.
This body's made of Earthly mud,
But *I* am *more* than flesh and blood.

Heaven and Earth abide in me
Until, from clay, one day, I'm free.
Then, at wedding number three,
A *heav'nly union*, we will be!

When I breathe, I breathe for *two*—
I can feel, my breath *is you!*
One, in body, *one,* in soul—
Truly, God has made us whole!

45. More and More

Charles Santiago, 5/12/23

Sweetheart, with the passing time,
More and more, our love's sublime.
You and I have found our niche.
By God's *grace,* we've struck it rich!

I am learning, more and more,
I have *passed* through heaven's door.
Sweetheart, when we said "I do,"
God took hold of me and you.

Dear, I cherish *this,* our bond.
How I love when you respond!
More and more, I see how you
Stick to me with heav'nly glue.

Stick to me, my whole life through.
I have nothing more to do
Than live this life, my dear, with you.
More and more, our love proves true.

46. You're Not Gone, 5/12/23

I can feel you feeling me—
Me, your bumbling bumblebee.
Heavens! Darling, let's proceed.
A word from you is all I need.

*I can feel you feeling me—
A living couple, dear, are we.
How I love you, bumblebee!
Let's proceed to ecstasy!*

Ecstasy is *You and Me*.
How I love this harmony!
You're not *gone*, and *you're* not *dead*.
Dear, let's go, full steam ahead!

*As you see, my Earthly beau—
No matter where on Earth you go—
We've a love that will not end.
Believe me, you're my dearest friend!*

My *other self*, are *you*, my love—
I know **what** I'm **speaking of!**
When I think I'm all alone,
You *call* me *on* our *telephone*.

YOU are never far from me—
More and more, this truth, I see.
Use our heav'nly telephone.
Never, dear, are you alone.

47. Embrace Me, Dear

Charles Santiago, 5/12/23

I'm no fool, dear. I can see
You are walking next to me.
Heaven's not a place in space.
Heaven, dear, is our embrace.

Embrace me, dear, and I will be
A happy, bumbling bumblebee.
Though you're on the "other side,"
It's *in* my *heart,* dear, *you abide.*

I have learned a lot, my love,
Since we bought that home, above—
I have died, and live with you,
Above this crazy Timbuktu.

Now and then, I cry, my dear,
Living in our home, down here.
By and by, I'll cry, no more,
Here, this side of heaven's door.

48. Reason to Crow, 5/13/23

Though I live up here, "above,"
Darling, you're the one I love.
Of course, it's SO, my Earthly beau—
Our love survived the mortal blow!
I walk with you, down there, "below,"
JUST because I love you SO.
IT'S the THING I love to do.
FOREVER, I'm in love with you!
We have reason, dear, to crow—
We've CONQUERED DEATH, and, true love, know.
Believe me, dear, we ONWARD go.
Can't you feel that WE still GROW?

These Earthly eyes keep fooling me!
Oh, for eyes, my love, *to see!*
Of course, the love we shared, down here,
Could *never,* darling, disappear.
Since, from flesh, we've been unpaired,
We've been brave, dear. We have dared—
Dared believe that you and I
Share a love that cannot die.
We have found, by God's dear grace,
A place where we meet, face-to-face.
True love, *yes,* my dear, we know.
Though you're "gone," I *feel* us *grow.*

49. Heaven's Light, 5/13/23

Kanapaha Botanical Gardens waterfall
Gainesville, Florida

*Take your pen, my love, and write
Rhymes that speak of heaven's light—
Heaven's light that shines on you
Till your life, down there, is through.*

*In this light that shines on you,
Feel, my dear, our love, so true.
We are blended in this light—
A lovely, Earthly/heav'nly sight.*

*I have brought you here, today—
Brought you here, through heaven's sway.
Heaven's light is shining, love,
On our union, here above.*

*In your life down there, below,
You're my lovely Earthly beau.
Heaven's light unites us, dear,
Down below, and WAY UP HERE.*

50. Oh, the Joys We Share!

Charles Santiago, 5/13/23
Kanapaha Botanical Gardens
Hummingbird garden
Gainesville, Florida

Once again, my heav'nly belle,
You have taught me, oh, so *well*—
I have died, and live with *you*,
Above this Earthly Timbuktu.

Just as true, my heav'nly bride,
You live *here*, right *by* my *side*.
Oh, the joys we share, my love,
Here, below, and *there*, above!

In and out of time and space,
Dear, we share this special grace.
We have *fooled* Man's *ancient foe*.
We have told him where to go!

I **stand amazed**, this day, my dear;
For, *it* is *you* who *brought* me *here!*
A garden's *such* a special place
To meet, my darling, face-to-face!

51. A Perfect Ending to a Perfect Day

Charles Santiago, 5/13/23
Back home from Kanapaha Botanical Gardens

My hand, my dear, I place in yours,
Because, *this day*, our love endures.
Hand in hand, we make our way,
Together, though I'm still in clay.
Man and wife, we still abide—
An Earthly groom and heav'nly bride.
I'm as *happy as* can *be*
To be your bumbling bumblebee.
A *garden,* dear, you brought me to—
A feat performed, alone, by you.

"*Dead and Gone,*" I know, so well,
Itself, has died, and gone to "hell."
I'd be lying, through and through,
If *I* claimed *"Dead and Gone"* were **true**.
"*Alive and Here,*" the song you sing,
Crowns me, dear, a *heav'nly* king!
I walked, today, with you, *above,*
Tasting, *here,* your heav'nly love.
"*Resurrection from the dead,*"
Again, rings clearly in my head.

52. Kanapaha Joy, 5/14/23

Rejoice with me, my Earthly beau!
ETERNAL union, dear, we know.
You and I don't need to wait
FOR some FUTURE meeting date.
TODAY, we're walking, hand in hand.
Life on Earth's our heav'nly land.
YOU, IN ME, AND I, IN YOU,
Hallows life in Timbuktu.
WE can SEE God's WORK on Earth—
Oh, how souls have HEAV'NLY worth!

I'm rejoicing, bumblebee,
In YOUR responding, dear, to me!
Life, AS ONE, is our delight,
Sharing NOW, dear, heaven's light!
Death and pain are now passé.
WE have found a higher way.
You can kiss your fears goodbye.
Our home is in the by-and-by.
Walk with me, dear, all your life.
We're, FOREVER, man and wife!

53. Lovely Gardens, Shining Bright

Charles Santiago, 5/15/23

I am you, and you are me,
Sets me free, my dear, to be
Ready for that final day,
Walking in this Earthly way.

Night and day will then be through,
As I *croon,* dear, *"you, you, you!"*
In the stillness of the night,
I'll escape to heaven's light.

Hand in hand, and side by side,
In heaven's light, we'll both abide.
Lovely gardens, shining bright,
Will fill us, dear, with pure delight!

As below, dear, *so,* above—
Gardens are our special love.
Below, we heard the Serpent's hiss!
Above, we taste unsullied bliss!

Peace and love will reign, supreme.
Life on Earth will seem a dream.
We'll rejoice, forever, dear,
Absent from the chaos, *here.*

54. This Path We've Trod, 5/15/23

Close your eyes and concentrate.
Angels wait at heaven's gate.
Show them you are game, my dear,
To leave the Earth and come UP HERE.
Sweet communion is ours, my love,
In heaven's lovely land, above.

There's no need for us to wait.
TODAY, my dear, let's celebrate
Resurrection from the dead.
Dine with me on heaven's bread!
Draw, my dear, a heav'nly breath
And feel we're free from pain and death!

We are ONE, my bumblebee.
I *am* **you**, *and* **you** *are* **me**.
Entwine, with me, in heaven's embrace,
And we can speak, dear, face-to-face.
Dead and gone, you know I'm not!
Behold, my darling, what God has wrought!

How I love this path we've trod,
Walking, hand in hand, with God!
A loving father and mother, dear,
GOD PROVIDES for this LIFE, up HERE.
LIVE with ME. I'll LIVE with YOU.
Our love, my darling, is never through!

55. A Monster You Must Slay, 5/15/23

DEAD AND GONE is mighty strong;
Yet, WHAT he TEACHES is ALL dead WRONG.
HE'S a monster YOU must slay,
With all due haste, dear. Don't delay!
Even YOU, alive with me,
His unsuspecting dupe, can be!

IMAGINE, my darling bumblebee,
Walking, hand in hand, with me.
Now, BELIEVE it! My DEAR, it's TRUE.
With DEAD AND GONE, you MUST be through!
On YOU, I'm DEPENDING, my Earthly beau,
To slay that monstrous, Earthly foe.

Heaven is HERE for me and you—
HERE in our EARTHLY rendezvous.
CLOSER, dear, we'll ONLY be,
THAT DAY—at wedding number three!
Don't let people make you think
WE'RE not SHARING a heav'nly link!

56. We Are Free, 5/16/23

I keep finding, oh, my dear,
You can live with *me,* down here.
What on Earth, dear, can I say?
Death's no reason for dismay!
I am free to laugh with you.
We are free to rendezvous.
We are finding, more, each day,
Peace and joy amid Earth's fray.

God has granted you, my love,
To live DOWN THERE and HERE, above.
God has granted you and me
To live, still, as a unity.
Darling, live that Earthly life.
I am, still, your loving wife.
How I thrill with you, below,
WHEN you THRILL to heaven's glow!

I'm a knight, in Earth's bleak day.
Chivalry *leads* me *on* my *way.*
I'm a slave to love, my dear,
Freed by finding you still here.
I'm a fool—by science, scorned—
Believing you've, my life, adorned.
I'm a corpse within a tomb,
Yet, *freed* from *death* and *freed* from *gloom.*

"*I* am **not** this **body**—no!"
Sing it, as a song, my beau!
"To the grave, I **will** not **go**."
I'm so glad, this truth, you know!
You and I are ONE, my love,
Down, below, and HERE, above.
Bodies DIE, but spirits LIVE
The ONE true LIFE that God can give!

57. Heaven's Lovely Glow, 5/17/23

Lovely mem'ries, dear, we share,
OF that EARTHLY life, down there.
Let them spur you on, my love,
TO this home we share, above.
Don't be blind and think that we,
Only, in the PAST, can BE.
Faith and love, my bumblebee,
TO our present link, are KEY.
Believe "I'm YOU, and YOU are ME,"
And share our love's pure ecstasy.
Walk, with me, this brand-new life
Of Earthly groom and heav'nly wife.
Gaze UP HERE, my Earthly beau,
Heav'nly secrets, dear, to know.

P.S., **dear**, I **love** you **so**,
AS we EVER, onward, GO.
Our bungalow on Earth, below,
Shines with heaven's lovely glow!

58. What a Gift!

Charles Santiago, 5/17/23

A sunbathing poem

Fearful, dear, I need not be,
That *there's* an *end* to *You* and *Me*.
God has shown—and *you* have, too—
We will *ever* rendezvous!
Wedding number two, my dear,
Has *shown* me *that* we *both* live *here*—
Here, below, and *here*, above—
Joined by everlasting love.

Faith and love have rescued me.
From the *grief* of death, I'm free!
No need, was there, to shed a tear;
But *I* was **robed** in **darkness**, **here**.
What a gift we've found, my love,
Fitting, now, like hand in glove!
Oh, my dear, what *will* it *be*—
That joy of wedding number three?

Sweetheart, here's my earnest plea—
More and more, that I would see
Pleasures, shared by you and me,
Filling us with ecstasy!
I'm your beau, your Earthly man,
Declaring, always, "Yes, we can!"
Our union, dear, is *not* by chance.
What a gift—*divine* romance!

59. I'm Content

Charles Santiago, 5/17/23

Greenwise Market
Tallahassee, Florida

I'm content, my heav'nly belle,
Because I *know* you, oh, so *well!*
I'm content because I *know*
We continue, dear, to grow.
I'm content to live this life,
Still, my dear, as man and wife.

In a rush, my dear, I'm *not*.
A **lot** of **patience**, **I** have **got**.
Alive, or dead, we make a pair,
Way down *here,* or way up *there*.
I thank **God***,* my **dear***,* for **you**
And our eternal rendezvous!

There's a **lot** I **do** not **know**
Of *how* it *is* that *we* still *grow*.
I'm *content,* myself, my dear,
As long as I can *feel* you *here*.
We have grown, in love, *a lot*—
Dying hasn't been for naught!

How I love to say, each day:
"I **love** you, **dear***,* in **every way***.*
I'm so *glad* I *met* you, *dear,*
That fateful day, that fateful year,
Way down *here* where *we began*
TO LIVE—with *me,* your biggest fan!"

61

60. Let Us Rejoice, 5/17/23

Response to poem 59. "I'm Content"

*And **lo**, I am **with** you, **forever**, my **dear**.*
*Every **day** on the **Earth**, dear, to **you**, I'll **appear**.*
***Forsaken**, my **darling**, you **never** will **be**.*
*Our **bond** is God-**given**. From **fear**, dear, be **free**!*
*A **heavenly** couple, this **instant**, we **are**—*
*From each **other**, my **dear**, we will **never** be **far**.*
***How** can I **say** it, my **dear**, so you'll **know**?*
*God **means** for us **always**, my **darling**, to **grow**!*
*You're a **temple**, my **darling**, in **which** I **abide**.*
*A **dwelling**, are **you**, dear, in **which** I **reside**.*
*Not a **moment** goes **by**, in your **life** on the **Earth**,*
*When **we** are not **slated** for **heavenly** mirth.*
***Heaven** is **here**, and **heaven** is **now**!*
***Worship** our **Maker** and, rev'rently, **bow**.*
***Let** us **rejoice** in our **Maker**, my **love**,*
*There, on the **ground**, and **here**, up **above**!*

61. Oh, the Joy That Death Can Bring!

Charles Santiago, 5/18/23

Completely free from every tear—
Help me reach that goal, my dear!
A single tear of grief makes clear
I believe that you're not here!
Heaven cannot enter in
If *Dead and Gone* is still my sin.

Dead and Gone, you wicked foe!
I despise you, head to toe!
And yet, my dear, I've come so far—
At least, I merit a golden star!
Peace will triumph within my breast
When *Dead and Gone* is put to rest.

We are victors, dear heav'nly belle.
Heav'nly secrets, we both can tell.
Death, itself, can serve, for us,
As tickets to a heav'nly bus.
Oh, the joy that death can bring—
Teaching mortals, God's praise, to sing!

How I love, each day, to crow:
"*I* am **not** this **body**—**no!**
To the **grave**, I **will** not **go!**
My body, though, must stay below."
Hand in hand, my heav'nly belle,
We've escaped this Earthly hell.

62. No Greater Thrill

Charles Santiago, 5/18/23

Of course, it's *so*. Of course, it's *so!*
More and more, it proves so *true*.
From my *side*, you didn't go.
I am living, *still*, with you!

We have found eternal life,
As we dare to intertwine.
I can *tell* you're still my wife.
We are *joined* by love, divine!

The *more* I leave the world behind me,
Oh, my dear, the *more* I find,
Heaven helps us now to be,
In the spirit, *more* aligned.

No greater thrill, my dear, have I,
As I *bumble* here, below,
Than learning, *here*, how *not* to cry;
For, dear, I share your heav'nly glow.

63. Not Alone

Charles Santiago, 5/19/23

I have *found* a river of life,
Flowing through this soul of mine,
Flowing like a liquid knife,
Flowing from a source, divine.

I have found a strange, new road.
It speaks, and takes me by the hand.
This road is, somehow, my abode;
Yet, leads me to a distant land.

I have found I'm not alone,
Though I *were* Earth's *only* man.
I *hear* a *lovely* dial tone,
Connecting me to heaven's clan.

I *feel* you, *darling,* by my side.
I'm happy, more than words can say.
My everlasting, lovely bride—
You *walk beside* me, *come what may!*

64. Our Past, 5/19/23

Our Earthly life's alive, UP HERE!
Our Earthly life can't disappear.
The core of who we are, my dear,
Began, one lovely Earthly year.

The past isn't dead, my Earthly beau.
Our life, back then, we still can know.
AS we, EVER, onward, go,
The past is part of how we grow.

The precious love we had, back then,
EVER, abides within our ken.
Remember, dear, our cozy den.
Intone, with me, to God, "Amen!"

For, **God***, my precious bumblebee,*
Reached down to Earth, to you and me;
And gave us sight, with which to see,
Our past began eternity.

65. No Need to Wait, 5/20/23

I'm delighting, dear, in you,
Till your Earthly days are through.
Delight in me, my bumblebee.
Share, with me, pure ecstasy!
Walk with me in HEAVEN'S way,
And WE'LL ENJOY each EARTHLY day.
God *desires US to see,*
We are, still, a unity.

Love will be our light and life,
Guiding us, as man and wife.
Love will show, my Earthly beau,
RESURRECTION LIFE, we know.
Every day, you'll see, my dear,
WE are ONE, down THERE and HERE.
WHAT a GIFT, my love, we share—
Heaven, HERE, and heaven, THERE!

People think that heaven's *far—*
Far beyond some shining star.
Oh, my darling, we have found
Heaven, *here,* right *on* the *ground!*
Since you died, my darling, *I*
Have seen our union cannot die.
And, dear, it's ecstasy to see
No need, to wait, in heaven, to be!

66. I Have Come

Charles Santiago, 5/21/23

Lake Kissimmee State Park
Lake Wales, Florida

I have come, in time and space,
Seeking for a special grace—
Grace, O God, to find the one,
To me, who is a shining sun.

Grant, O Father of the light,
She and I may find delight,
In and out of time and space,
By Your grace, God, face-to-face.

Ruler of the day and night,
Grant, I pray, the gift of sight.
Heaven's glory, may I see,
Shining deep inside of me.

One, You made us—*so,* to be—
Friends, for all eternity.
Ruler of the land and sea,
Set us, from Earth's darkness, free.

67. I Am Trusting You Will Be, 5/21/23

Lake Kissimmee State Park
Lake Wales, Florida

Today, you called me "bumblebee,"
Reminding me, from death, we're free.
When I think you're *gone*, my dear,
Forgive me—*I'm* half *blind*, down *here*.

Though you're, now, my *heav'nly* wife,
Still, you share my *Earthly* life.
I'm astounded we can share
A life, down *here,* and one, up *there!*

I'm delighted, bumblebee,
YOU believe in YOU AND ME.
WHAT a love this IS, we share!
It's because, my dear, you DARE!

DARE believe in me, my love,
And we'll enjoy our home, ABOVE.
*I am trusting **you** will be*
As busy as a bumblebee.

68. Join Me on the Other Side! 5/21/23

Lake Kissimmee State Park
Lake Wales, Florida

Join me on the Other Side!
Claim me as your heav'nly bride!
I'VE claimed YOU, my Earthly beau.
Sweetheart, WE'RE all SET to GO!

WHY live BY YOURSELF, my dear?
We've GOT this PRECIOUS home, "UP HERE!"
DEAD AND GONE is SO untrue!
EVERY DAY, I'm THERE with YOU!

*How I **love** our rendezvous!*
YOU know, dear, that WE'RE not THROUGH!
Heaven's helping me and you,
TO our VOWS, dear, to be true.

When you play our songs of love,
I'M so THRILLED, up here, ABOVE!
Join me on the Other Side!
Meet with me, your heav'nly bride!

69. Sharing Heaven's Glow, 5/22/23

Lake Kissimmee State Park
Lake Wales, Florida

As I walk down here, below,
Sweetheart, I can feel us grow.
Heaven's not a *place* to go—
Heaven is, *the truth,* to know!

Truth be told, my heav'nly belle,
Life, below, is mighty swell.
When you died, I *went* to *hell,*
But, now, I'm feeling more than well.

Let's proceed, forever, dear.
I am *smiling,* ear to ear.
Your lovely voice, I've learned to hear,
Filling me with heav'nly cheer.

Once again, my Earthly beau,
A trip on Earth has served, to show,
WE are sharing heaven's glow.
Heaven is, THIS LOVE, to know!

70. A Garden, 5/22/23

The view behind 'El Retiro'
Orion W. (Bill) Fraiser memorial bench
Bok Tower Gardens
Lake Wales, Florida

THINK, my darling. Think, REAL HARD—
Not only EARTH, but HEAVEN, regard.
DO you THINK our life, BEFORE,
Is ALL we had—and nothing more?

NO, my dear. Incline your ear.
Listen, hard, my voice, to hear.
You and I, today, have MORE—
Above the Earth, we now can soar!

Soar with me, above your clay.
WE have ACCESS to HEAVEN'S day!
All the joy we shared, on Earth,
Is now surpassed by heav'nly mirth!

The beauty, now, before your eyes,
Is part of heaven's great surprise—
Sweetheart, YOU don't HAVE to DIE,
To meet with me "above the sky."

Rest assured, my bumblebee—
YOU are NEVER far from me!
A GARDEN, though, my Earthly beau,
Is filled with heav'nly joy, to know.

71. A Better Place

Charles Santiago, 5/22/23

Bok Tower Gardens
Lake Wales, Florida

Mr. Bok, you placed your grave
At the *foot* of heaven's tower.
It's a *sight* my mind will save
Till my *own* last, Earthly hour.

Thank you, sir, for *such* a sight.
It humbled me and made me feel
A strong desire to seek the light
That fills the heart with holy zeal.

I will try to live like you—
To leave the world, a better place.
In *all* I think and say and do,
I'll *try* to *help* the human race.

What a *gift*, to us, you gave—
A paradise that thrills the soul!
To selfishness, I'll *be* no *slave*.
I'll *seek* a *higher,* heav'nly goal!

72. What Better Place? 5/23/23

Lake Kissimmee State Park
Lake Wales, Florida

In this world we've found, my dear,
Way down THERE and way up HERE,
THERE'S no NEED to be afraid.
Everything, by love, is made.

I have called you "bumblebee."
You're so busy seeking me!
Bumble, darling. I will be,
ALWAYS, dear, right NEXT to THEE.

Like I said, cast fear aside.
I delight to be your bride.
What began on good old Earth,
Continues, HERE, with heav'nly mirth!

A "ladybug," you've called me, love,
AS you MAKE your way ABOVE.
A ladybug and bumblebee—
A perfect couple, we will be!

What BETTER place for us to meet—
To make this love we share, complete—
Than THERE, where Mr. Edward Bok,
A GARDEN, made, where we can talk?

73. Heavenly Ties, 5/23/23

Rain shelter by the Exedra
Bok Tower Gardens
Lake Wales, Florida

I'm remote, my Earthly beau,
Only if you THINK it's so.
Learn to feel my heav'nly glow,
Every day, down there, "below."

THINK—and tell me, bumblebee,
Could we really, TRULY, be
A DISJOINT BEING, you and me?
RIGHT NOW, dear, we're a UNITY!

Don't let matter cloud your eyes.
Don't lose sight of heav'nly ties.
Let OTHERS say their sad goodbyes.
TO the heavens, dear, be wise.

Imagine me, dear, by your side,
STILL, a faithful, loving bride.
IN YOU, my darling, I'll confide:
"By DEATH, we've BEEN more UNIFIED!
It's JUST the BODY, dear, that died!
*I remember **how** you **cried!***
NOW let HEAVEN be your guide
To show how you, IN ME, abide."

74. Our Mighty, Peaceful Bond

Charles Santiago, 5/23/23

Francis and Mildred Hubbard memorial bench
By the reflection pond
Bok Tower Gardens
Lake Wales, Florida

Darling, I'm so *one* with you,
I'm *adrift* in Timbuktu.
I *feel* like *such* a stranger *here*,
And, yet, I *feel* no danger *here*.

Here, at the reflection pond,
I *feel* our mighty, peaceful bond.
We never said goodbye, my dear.
That's *why* I *feel* you, *still*, down here.

Two worlds—my lovely, heav'nly belle—
Two worlds, we live in—I can tell!
What's a year, or more, down here?
Wedding number three is near!

The great Bok Tower is striking five,
Reminding me that we're alive,
In and *out* of time and space,
Communing still, dear, face-to-face.

We don't need mere Earthly clay
To rendezvous by night or day.
I'm so *glad* that you and I,
Today, have found the by-and-by!

75. More than Memories, 5/24/23

Lake Kissimmee State Park
Lake Wales, Florida

More than mem'ries—by God's design—
We are sharing, dear love of mine.
More and more, I feel it's true—
You are **me**, and **I** am **you**.

I concentrate on *you*, each day,
And, *thus*, discover heaven's sway.
I never would have guessed that we,
So united, *still*, could be.

Heaven, dear, is WHERE YOU ARE—
NOT beyond some lofty star.
YOU don't have to die, my dear,
With ME, in heaven, to appear.

Why, my darling, live alone?
Why, in mis'ry, moan and groan?
Delight in me, and you will see,
WE are joined, in ecstasy!

76. O Great Resurrection Day!

Charles Santiago, 5/24/23

Lake Kissimmee State Park
Lake Wales, Florida

O Great Resurrection Day,
Raising me from Earthly clay,
I can *feel* your rays of light,
Filling me with pure delight!

From the dead, I'm raised on high,
While this body still must die.
Resurrection Day, you shine
Deep within this heart of mine!

Heaven comes to walk with me,
Shining light, so *I* can *see*,
Resurrection Day is *here*,
Filling me with heav'nly cheer!

People think that *they* must *wait*—
Wait for some great, future date—
To pass through heaven's lovely gate
And find a peaceful, holy state.

O Great Resurrection Day,
I can *feel* your holy sway.
Heaven's *here*—before I die.
I'll rejoice, and ask not why.

77. Oh, What Joy a Garden Brings!

Charles Santiago, 5/24/23

Pine Ridge Preserve Trail
Bok Tower Gardens
Lake Wales, Florida

It's been a wondrous trip, my dear,
Coming to this garden, here.
Oh, what joy a garden brings!
Deep inside, my spirit sings:

> I'm in heaven, though on Earth.
> A garden brings such heav'nly mirth!
> Oh, my Maker, *how* I *love*
> To walk the lovely streets, above.
> These few short years on Earth, below,
> To some, are filled with grief and woe.
> I'm so glad, this joy, I've found,
> While, to this Earth, my feet are bound!
> For Mr. Edward Bok, I pray,
> Gladness, *there,* in heaven's day.
> *What* a gift, to us, he gave,
> Before his body found its grave!
> Thank you, Mr. Edward Bok,
> *For* this *lovely,* heav'nly walk!

The gift God gave, to you and me,
Is—walking, hand in hand, to see
The beauties of eternity,
Experienced in our unity!

78. Imagine, 5/24/23

Gordon A. Cain memorial bench
Next to the singing tower
Bok Tower Gardens
Lake Wales, Florida

Imagine ME, my Earthly beau.
Imagine ME, your heav'nly belle.
*Imagine **how** I **love** you **so**,*
To send my love by sound of bell.
Listen to these bells, so pure—
Of Earthly ills, the heav'nly cure.
Imagine you and me, my love,
At home, as ONE, in heaven, above.

Imagine THERE, on Earth, below,
We ALSO live, as ONE, my dear.
It matters NOT, dear, WHERE you go,
Count on me. I'm always near.
Imagine that I didn't die.
Imagine there's no need to cry.
Rejoice, with me, my bumblebee,
And taste, with me, eternity!

Sweet music, from the singing tower,
Joins us, NOW, in love, divine!
Sweet music, by your awesome power,
TO the Almighty, our souls, incline.
Go, my darling, on your way,
Thankful that we had this day.
Imagine, darling, you and me,
Partners for eternity!

79. Beyond What Words Can Tell

Charles Santiago, 5/24/23

Bok Tower Gardens
Lake Wales, Florida

Darling, *I* must *say* it's true:
You can *feel* me *feeling you,*
And *I* can *feel* you *feeling me.*
A ladybug and bumblebee,
We can *feel* our unity.

But *also,* dear, I *must* say, *too*—
Circumstance leads *me* to *you.*
Not only do I *feel* you, dear,
But, *in* the *things* that happen *here,*
You *prove* to *me* that *you* are *near.*

Dear, we've come a long, long way
Since that fateful, woeful day.
The gardens, here, my heav'nly belle,
Today, have shown me, oh, *so well,*
We *live beyond* what words can tell!

80. Light from Heaven, 5/25/23

Lake Kissimmee State Park
Lake Wales, Florida

Sealed, as one, forever, dear,
Though YOU'RE down THERE, and I'M up HERE—
SO, it IS, my Earthly beau,
AS we, ever, onward, go.

Light, from heaven, IS our GUIDE,
Keeping us, my dear, in stride.
However many days are yours,
Be assured, our love endures.

*I am **yours**, dear bumblebee,*
For NOW, and for eternity.
That happy day we tied the knot,
Is NOW and, EVER, what GOD has WROUGHT.

ETERNAL joy, is ours, my love,
IN a MANSION, up here above.
WHEN your body can go, no more,
YOU'LL walk THROUGH our mansion door!

81. More than Clay, 5/26/23

Don't be blind, my Earthly beau—
Life is more than what's below.
AND, my darling bumblebee,
Don't be blind to YOU AND ME!

Trust YOUR SOUL to find the way.
Darling, we are more than CLAY!
Trust in me, each Earthly day,
Even, when the skies are gray.

A gift, God gave to me and you—
This Earthly/heav'nly rendezvous.
The world will say our life is through,
All, UNAWARE of heav'nly glue!

WHATEVER happens THERE, below,
Remember, you're my Earthly beau.
This life I live, each day, with you,
Will never, EVER, dear, be through!

82. We Found Eternity! 5/26/23

My darling, when your days are through,
We'll continue, me and you.
FOREVER, we'll go on our way—
ONE, my dear, just like today.

Torn apart, we CANNOT be.
***I** am **you**, and **you** are **me**.*
Dear, we found eternity—
A ladybug and bumblebee.

On the day your body dies,
It will come as no surprise,
Side by side, my dear, we'll be,
AGLOW at wedding number three!

Now, my darling Earthly beau,
This Earthly/heav'nly row, we'll hoe.
I'M enjoying YOU, my love,
AS you journey here, above!

83. A Higher Life

Charles Santiago, 5/26/23

The rhymes we write seem true, to me,
Reflecting sweet eternity.
Our union, dear, gives birth to rhymes
To help me through these Earthly times.
More and more, I sense you, dear,
As *though* you *still* live, *with* me, *here.*
Eternal life, we share, my love,
Down *here,* below, and *there,* above.

When our Earthly days are through—
Oh, my dear, I've learned from you—
Just the Earthly body *ends.*
Our soul ascends, to meet with friends.
Ascending and descending, *we,*
With *all* our loved ones, then, can *be.*
Dear, I *know* these *things* are *so,*
For, *you* and *I* still, *onward,* go.

I'm *living,* now, a higher life,
Holding hands with you, my wife.
How I've *changed,* my heav'nly belle,
Beyond the power of words to tell!
I'm so *thrilled,* rememb'ring when
We watched *movies* in our den!
"Boy meets girl"—That's you and me,
Sweethearts for eternity!

84. Oh, the Joy, to Be, *as ONE!*

Charles Santiago, 5/27/23

You have found me, dear, I know.
I can *feel* your heav'nly glow!
Oh, the joy, to be, *as ONE*,
Shining like a mighty sun!
God has given, you and me,
Life, for all eternity!
When we said "I do," *down here,*
God, *above,* our vows, did hear.
Dear, our Maker loves us *so,*
Saving us from mankind's foe!

How I *love* to live with you!
Forever, we are *one,* not *two!*
Thirty years, *down here,* my love,
Won, for us, a home *above!*
How I *love* to reminisce
Of times, down here, when *we* would *kiss!*
Yes, it's true—Those times, I miss—
Though we're sharing heav'nly bliss.
Now, I wait for ecstasy—
Ours, at wedding number three!

85. Your Faith, 5/27/23

A sunbathing poem

Let OTHERS say their sad goodbyes—
WE'LL rely on heav'nly ties.
Dear, our love is far too great
For, either you or me, to wait
Until your Earthly body dies,
For us, our love, to realize.

"AS your FAITH, so SHALL it BE"—
DEAR, this IS our MAGIC KEY!
Darling, STILL, believe in me!
We'll unite in ecstasy!
Dear, your faith has set us free.
God has granted us our plea!

*You **know** **me**, and **I** know **you**.*
WE both KNOW our LOVE'S not THROUGH!
***SIGNS**, I send you—Yes, it's true,*
To help us in our rendezvous.
*But, **SIGNS**, or **NOT**, dear, HERE'S a CLUE—*
*The **SUBSTANCE** is our life, **ANEW**!*

86. I Feel You Near

Charles Santiago, 5/28/23

Darling, though I'm missing you,
I find, each day, our love's not through.
We have learned to rendezvous.
Our love is proving to be true.

Like a child who loves to read,
In my mind, I mount a steed
And speed away—my *heart,* to *heed*—
From *Earthly sorrow, to* be *freed.*

I admit—It's *hard,* my dear.
I'm so *prone* to *doubt* and *fear.*
So often, though, I feel you near,
And all my doubts then disappear.

Yes, this war is being won.
Heav'nly joys have, now, begun.
Oh, how *sweet,* to feel we're *ONE,*
Though, with *Earthly clay,* you're *done!*

87. Three Weddings

Charles Santiago, 5/28/23

A sunbathing poem

You *gave* yourself to *me,* my dear,
At weddings, numbers one and two.
And every day I live, down here,
I *give* myself, my dear, to *you.*

In wedding number one, my love,
God *gave us* a brand-new life.
For wedding two, you flew above,
While *we remained,* dear, *man* and *wife.*

Remember how I *used* to *say*:
"Oh, a wedding—what *delight!*
How I love a wedding day!
Souls, made *one,* dear—what a sight!"

Souls, made *one,* my dear, are *we,*
Though you've *finished out* your day.
A ladybug and bumblebee,
We've *learned* to *move,* to heaven's sway!

How I love a wedding day—
Two souls, *joined* in *unity!*
Dear, I'll *leave* this mortal clay
For *you* and wedding number three!

88. My Creed

Charles Santiago, 5/28/23

Whole Foods Market
Tallahassee, Florida

I will *seek* you *here, today!*
I will *find* you, *come what may!*
Though we've come a long, long way,
I still *have* to *fight* this *clay!*

These eyes of clay are hard to fight.
Every day, they cause me fright.
"She's *gone*," they say. "She's out of sight,
Living in a land, so bright."

This I know, my heav'nly bride—
It's *just* the *body*, dear, that died.
In the spirit, we abide,
Still a couple, side by side.

This *very* day, in Timbuktu,
I can *walk* and *talk* with you.
Darling, we can bill and coo!
Our love, we're free, to still pursue!

All these *truths* make *up* my *creed*,
And *I* have *learned* they're true, indeed!
It's *like* we're *now* a brand–new breed—
From *death* and *sorrow, we've* been *freed!*

89. Remember to Recite Our Creed, 5/28/23

Inspired by the music "Belonging" by Michele McLaughlin

Lafayette Heritage Trail Park
Tallahassee, Florida

DO not THINK you're all alone.
Don't THINK you're THERE, dear, BY YOURSELF.
*What TRAGEDY, to THINK that's **SO!***
*Think, instead, dear—WE are **ONE!***
*I am **with** you every day.*
THERE'S no NEED, my dear, to WAIT!
Our happiness is NOW complete.
Believe me, dear, I didn't LEAVE!
APART, my dear, we COULDN'T be!
*I am **you**, and **you** are **me!***

*I **love** this **life** we **share**, my dear.*
*I **live in you**, and always will!*
*Remember **to** recite our creed—*
*This **creed**, **BY DEATH**, we **came** to **heed!***

90. Eternal Union, 5/29/23

In and out of time and space,
WE can speak, dear, face-to-face.
THROUGH the HEAVENS and ON the EARTH,
We are, dear, each other's mirth.

Let's rejoice in words SO TRUE:
*"**You** are **me**, and **I** am **you**!"*
Death, our union, cannot break!
Death, our vows, cannot unmake!

Thirty Earthly years, my dear,
Were NICE—but WE belong "up here."
FEEL, my love, eternity—
***I** am **you**, and **you** are **me**!*

***How** I **love** you, through and through!*
WE have found a life that's true.
Death, we've found, was JUST A DOOR.
Our Maker, dear, let US ADORE!

THERE below, in time and space,
Share, with me, our special grace—
ETERNAL UNION, bumblebee.
***I** am **you**, and **you** are **me**!*

91. A Ladybug and Bumblebee

Charles Santiago, 5/29/23

I was *there,* my heav'nly bride,
The day your Earthly body died.
And *now* I find you're *here,* with me,
Having dubbed me, "bumblebee."

In our union, I abide,
Rememb'ring, dear, that day you died.
Oh, my dear, you *now* reside
Within my heart, my heav'nly bride!

We are walking *now,* my love,
In heaven, *here*—and *there,* "above."
I am *thrilled* to walk with you
Until these Earthly days are through!

Heavens! Dear, what *will* it *be*—
That wondrous wedding number three?—
A ladybug and bumblebee,
From Day and Night, completely free!

92. A Door

Charles Santiago, 5/30/23

Blind men think that loved ones die
And live beyond the Earthly sky.
I was blind, but now I see—
Those in love, from death, are free!
Oh, how *needless*—tears of grief!
Death is *not* a monstrous thief!
Death, for lovers, is a door
To realms that they can then explore—
One, below, and one, above—
Both infused with heav'nly love.
Oh, for eyes, to *always* see,
Love is for eternity!

Dear, I *feel* you *in* my *soul!*
Love has made, of us, one whole!
I don't *have* to **die**, my love,
To live with you in heaven above!
Death—you *phantom!*—Where's your sting?
You're, to me, a conquered thing!
I have *left* you in the ring,
Knocked out COLD, a ruined king!
Let this Earthly body *die*
Below the beauty of the sky!
Sweetheart, we have found a way
To live in heaven, *now, TODAY!*

93. This Union

Charles Santiago, 5/30/23

What a *gift*—my love, my life—
This *union*, joining you and me!
When I *took* you, *as* my *wife*,
I was **blind** as I could be!

Way back *then*, my ladybug,
Darkness was a friend of mine.
Earthly pleasure *was* my *drug*.
Oh, *what darkness, did* I s*hine*!

From **day one***,* my heav'nly belle,
I confessed that *you* were ***fine***.
From the *start*, dear, I could *tell*,
Heav'nly light, in you, *did shine*!

Heav'nly light, my heav'nly bride,
Shines around me *now,* I find.
You, within my heart, abide.
Dear, I *am*, no longer, *blind*!

What a *gift,* my dear, to see,
Here, below, where *I reside*—
God has joined us, you and me,
Forever, dear, as groom and bride!

94. You Haven't *Died* nor Have You *Left*

Charles Santiago, 5/30/23

Darling, here's a note, to say,
I *love* you, dear, in every way.
Knowing you are here, with me,
I'm learning, *frantic, not* to be.
What a trial death has been!
Still, you *are* my *closest* kin!
All my days, I'll love you, dear,
Until it's time to leave down here.

I *do* my *best,* ALONE, to be,
To, *better,* feel our unity.
Especially, dear, at eventide,
I can *feel* you *haven't* died,
Nor *have* you *left* and *gone away*—
No matter, dear, what *others* say!
How I *love* to feel your glow.
To feel your glow is, *life,* to know!

As I muse, my heav'nly belle,
I've *got* this *thought* I need to tell—
It seems, to me, our life, my dear,
Is, *little* meant, to be *down here.*
We are sharing life, *indeed,*
Above, where bodies do not bleed.
Patiently, I'll count the days
Until I'm done with Earthly ways.

95. Love Will See Us Through, 5/31/23

Remember when my body died,
And you will feel me by your side.
Our life continues to unfold,
If YOU, my dear, will be so bold,
To put your hand in mine
And trust in love divine.
Believe in God, believe in me,
And you, yourself, my dear, will see
That we will always be
A living unity.
Believe in love, my Earthly beau;
For, BY our LOVE, we've conquered woe.
A spooky ghost, my dear, I'm NOT—
It's you and I *who tied the knot.*
Now put your fears away.
Enjoy, with me, TODAY!
And if, my dear, you don't BELIEVE,
I'll play this card that's up my sleeve—
I'll pray, with all my might,
You'll conquer Earthly night
And see our heav'nly house
Where I abide, your spouse;
For if, my dear, you close your eyes,
We'll soon be saying sad goodbyes!
Don't close your eyes to love!
Live, with me, "above!"
I ***trust*** *in* ***you****, my bumblebee,*
To be, from doubt, completely free!
Love will see us through
All that you must do.

96. We Are *One*, It's True!

Charles Santiago, 5/31/23

All that *I* must *do*,
Is *live,* my love, for you;
For, *we* are ONE—It's true!
We never could be *two.*
That day your body died—
Oh, my dear, I cried!
Death, dear, did me in.
Blindness was my sin!
Our Maker joined us, you and me,
Forever, *ONE,* my dear, to be.
Death was just a door
We entered, to explore.
Earthly/heav'nly life, we share,
Because, my dear, *we dare!*
With my *pen,* my dear, I write
Words that help me pass the night.
Day or night, my heav'nly belle,
With this *pen,* I love to tell
How *you* and *I* have won
A life beyond Earth's sun!
A ladybug and bumblebee—
My dear, we found eternity!
As I *pen* this rhyme,
I'm *conscious* of that time
You *"left"* for heaven's shore,
Our Maker, to adore.
Angels *ruled,* that day!
Dear, I felt their sway!
Angels, *now,* are near.
How they *love* us, dear!

97. Our Heavenly Mirth! 5/31/23

You SEE, my darling, how it's true—
YOU'VE found ME, and I'VE found YOU!
Accept it, dear—It's HERE, to stay,
Until your final Earthly day.
You're so fearful I will leave!
Listen, dear: "Believe. BELIEVE!"
For thirty years, we walked on EARTH.
NOW accept our HEAV'NLY mirth!
Believe our bond is JUST as REAL
As ALL those THINGS, on Earth, you FEEL!
***I** don't **mean** to **chide** you, dear,*
But, sweetheart, YOU must LOSE this FEAR!
Why deprive us by your doubt?
Trust me, WE'VE got HEAV'NLY CLOUT.
Heaven's HERE, for you and me.
Don't FAIL me NOW, my bumblebee!

98. Be Wise! 6/1/23

*Dear, I **want** you **to** be **wise**.*
Don't be shocked at Man's demise.
It's JUST the BODY, dear, that dies.
Life goes on, beyond Earth skies.
It shouldn't be a big surprise—
LOOK how WE'VE maintained our ties!
Don't be fooled by Earthly eyes.
Things are JUST as YOU surmise—
Life goes on when spirits rise.
ETERNAL LIFE is Man's great prize!
A HIGHER life, men realize—
Witness how we've reached new highs.
After all your cries and sighs,
YOU'RE now WISE to Earthly lies.
THERE'S no NEED for sad goodbyes
WHEN, "the farm," a loved one "buys."
BY the LIGHT that heaven supplies,
WE see THROUGH the clay's disguise!

Be wise, my darling bumblebee—
Keep on walking, dear, with me!

99. Oh, How Sweet, This Bond of Ours!

Charles Santiago, 6/2/23

Darling, it is *you*, I *know!*—
Filling me with heaven's glow!
I can *feel* you *telling* me:
"*Welcome to eternity!*"
We are bound, AS ONE, my love,
Though you've "left" for heaven, "above."
You and I have died and won
Life beyond Earth's mighty sun!

Though I'm robed in Earthly clay,
I can *feel* your heav'nly sway.
Oh, how *sweet,* this bond of ours,
High above all Earthly powers!
Though I'm bound in Earthly skin,
I'm your *guest* in Heaven's Inn.
Angels have arranged this life,
Mindful, *we're* still *man* and *wife!*

As I *finish out* my *run,*
I'm *basking under HEAVEN'S* sun!
Death has made our love, my dear,
Expand beyond our home, down here.
We are *ONE,* in heaven above,
Learning how the angels love.
When my *days* on Earth are through,
We'll continue—me and you.

100. A Letter from Heaven, 6/2/23

We have learned a lot in 3 years and 10 months. We have GROWN a lot in 3 years and 10 months. We're in it for the "long haul," my dear. We have, forever and ever, to grow. Relax. Take it easy, my dear, and enjoy our journey through time. You believe in me—that I am not dead and not gone away. Let that faith continue to bring us together in your Earthly life. Learn to trust our spiritual union above the Earthly plane. It is IN YOU. "I am you, and you are me," can serve as a creed for us—especially now. When you are sad, it's because you are trying to be, and hoping to be, like we were BEFORE! It won't work, dear. Those days are gone. We must adapt to our new circumstances. Trust in our love, my darling. It has not dried up and disappeared—like a corpse would do! Trust IN ME. Trust in MY LOVE FOR YOU. Do not be blind and think that we are SEPARATED! You FEEL me, I know. Rejoice in THAT, my darling! I am not going away! We will not grow APART. It's so OBVIOUS, but the nature of the difference between us, now, makes these admonitions to you, my darling, valuable and encouraging because your Earthly side is so alienated from our spiritual reality. I love you, dear—like I always HAVE and always WILL. IMAGINE—if you HAVE to—my dear. IMAGINE me! You will link up to me because I am MORE than JUST in your imagination. Our ongoing union, my darling, is a wonder for the angels to behold—and a wonder, UNSPEAKABLE, for US to experience! If you didn't BELIEVE IN IT, my dear, it would never "get off the ground." Don't be afraid that others will label you as superstitious, gullible, unintelligent, or mentally unbalanced. WHAT OF IT, dear? What is more precious to you and me than YOU AND ME? Don't let your inability to totally understand our present union make you think that it is tenuous. Love, my darling, is the most beautiful thing there is! Let us BE that love, dear. Be A FOOL for it, dear! THAT is your greatest wisdom. You must rely on HOPE as well as LOVE FULFILLED. We HAVE, dear, but we also WILL HAVE what is GREATER. Don't worry that you can't quite wrap your Earthly consciousness around it. LIVE for our current love, my darling, and for our future reunion in our poetic "wedding number three." Hope, FULFILLED, and hope of a GREATER FULFILLMENT—Let the two be your daily bread. Our trips, our movies, our poems, our shared experience—They are our heaven, my dear. Listen to me, my Earthly beau: "I am not DEAD. I am not GONE. I am not a SPOOKY GHOST! I certainly, dear, do not love you LESS!" All my love to you, my one and only! Let us continue!

101. God Is Love, 6/3/23

WE can grow, my Earthly beau,
THROUGH the folks on Earth you know.
Darling, we are ONE with those
WHO, on Earth, wear HEAVEN'S CLOTHES.

Hermits, sometimes, cannot see
Light from heaven's fam'ly tree.
God is calling you—and me—
FRIENDS, with Earthlings, dear, to be.

Grow, my beau, in Earthly love
And sparkle HERE, in heaven above.
"God is love" means YOU must BE
*A **friendly**, Earthly bumblebee.*

TRUST that LOVE will GIVE, to you,
GRACE—to others, to be true.
THERE'S so MUCH that THEY can DO
To help US, dear, to bill and coo.

102. Come Fly with Me! 6/3/23

Ladybug, I live, today,
For, *You* and *I* have *found* our *way*.
I've escaped the dreadful clutch
Of *Dead and Gone's* deceitful touch.

What a scoundrel—*Dead and Gone*—
Filled with mighty, Earthly brawn!
I'm so glad I killed him, dead,
Nevermore, his might, to dread!

Ladybug, come fly with me—
Me, your Earthly bumblebee.
You're not *gone,* and *you're* not *dead!*
Dead and Gone, from us, has fled!

Come fly with me! COME FLY WITH ME,
My mighty, Earthly bumblebee!
You have killed that monster, dead,
Proving, dear, that we're still wed!

103. You Are Learning, 6/3/23

A sunbathing poem

Remember, darling bumblebee,
WE are STILL a unity.
YOU don't HAVE to worry, love—
I'VE not DISAPPEARED above!
*I am **trailing you**, my dear,*
Every day of every year.
Darling, don't be like THE REST.
Believe that death was JUST A TEST.
WE have LEARNED to carry on,
NOW, in heaven's lovely dawn.
So OFTEN, dear, you think I'm GONE—
YOU'RE the clothes that I have on!
Heaven's NOT, dear, when you die.
TODAY, we're in the by-and-by!
You are learning, I admit.
You're acquiring heav'nly wit.
It PAINS me WHEN you THINK we're THROUGH
When, EVERY DAY, I'm HERE with you!

Now, my darling Earthly beau,
LAUGH and SMILE, and WE will GO
Beyond the gloom of poet Poe.
Of HEAV'NLY UNION, we will crow!

104. A Happy Bumblebee

Charles Santiago, 6/3/23 (full moon)

A ladybug and bumblebee—
Darling, you and I are free—
Free from death and tragedy.
We're *SOARIN'* through eternity!

Every day, I learn anew,
Sweetheart, you and I aren't through!
If I *trusted* Earthly eyes,
I'd be *duped* by Earthly lies.

Since you flew through Earthly skies,
I have *grown* two *brand*-new *eyes*.
I can *see* our home, above,
Built, for us, by God's own love.

Sweetheart, listen, as I croon
Underneath a bright, full moon:
"I'm a happy bumblebee,
Awaiting wedding number three."

105. Matters of the Heart, 6/4/23

Matters of the heart, my love—
THEY'RE what MATTER, here "above."
Matters of the flesh, my dear,
Matter, not at all, "up here."
Love, my darling, made us ONE.
Eternal union, we have won.
It's plain enough for ALL to see—
*I am **you**, and **you** are **me**.*

Sweetheart, till your dying day,
We'll be walking heaven's way.
Proclaim, by dint of heav'nly brawn:
"DEAD AND GONE is dead and gone!"
We are walking, hand in hand,
NOW, my love, in heaven's land.
THERE, below Earth's pretty sky,
We enjoy the by-and-by!

Like I've said, dear: "Laugh and smile."
AFTER ALL—in JUST a while—
GONE, will be the Earthly life
While WE CONTINUE, man and wife.
WHAT a GIFT is ours, my love—
ETERNAL UNION, here "above!"
*I am **you**, and **you** are **me**,*
Now, and for eternity!

106. Wedding Bells, 6/5/23

Death did not remove me, dear,
FROM this HOME we share, down here.
Lovers don't just, UP and GO!
ETERNAL UNION, lovers know!

Death became, for you and me,
An entranceway to heav'nly glee!
Though it's hard, at times, to see,
We remain a unity.

Death tries hard to make you think,
Between us, there remains no link.
Have you felt me, dear, OR NOT,
Since our second wedding knot?

*I don't **mean** to chide you, dear.*
My aim is just to help you hear
Wedding bells, so loud and clear,
For wedding number three, UP HERE!

107. Our Niche, 6/5/23

A sunbathing poem

Our niche, my darling, we have found,
While I *trek* here, *on* the *ground.*
Dead and Gone, I fight, each day.
How I *wish* he'd *go away!*

Still, it's *more than life,* to know,
Even so, our love will grow!
After *all* we've *shared,* my dear,
Still, sometimes, I *just* don't *hear!*

Patience, have, with me, my love—
I'm *striving for* our home above;
Although this bungalow, below,
Is Eden when I *feel* your *glow!*

Your hearing, dear, is very good—
For which, **up here**, I **knock** on **wood**.
YOU have HEARD so MUCH from ME,
You've MORPHED in TO a bumblebee!

108. It's, *as If*

Charles Santiago, 6/5/23

I'm no *fool,* my heav'nly belle.
I'm no *fool,* for *I* can *tell,*
You and I are truly *ONE*
Though, your Earthly race, you've run.

Flesh and blood, I *do* not *need.*
Your heav'nly aura, *I* can *heed.*
It's, *as if,* you *haven't left,*
Because, my dear, *you HAVEN'T left!*

Oh, how *blind* these eyes can be
Though, dear, *I'm* a *bumblebee!*
Oh, what *heav'nly joy* I lose
Because I'm blind to heav'nly clues!

And, *yet,* my darling, *still,* I see
Heav'nly joys for you and me.
I'm no *fool,* my *heav'nly bride—*
I still *feel* you by my side!

109. Eventide, 1

Charles Santiago, 6/5/23

A sunset poem

Darling, as I read our rhymes,
I'm amazed at all the times
We have proved—to you and me—
Myst'ries of eternity!
Since you "flew" to heaven, "above,"
We've been living, hand in glove.
What pure *joy,* my dear, to know,
Life, *today,* as belle and beau!

Death has brought us *closer,* dear—
I can *feel* you, oh, so near!
Dear, I live for *only this*—
To walk with you in heav'nly bliss!
I'm astounded when I think
Upon the myst'ry of our link:
"*You* are *me,* and *I* am *you*"—
Holy words that ring so true!

What *delight,* my heav'nly bride—
To sit with you at eventide!
What great *joy* must *be, above,*
When *here, below,* we *share* such *love!*
Right NOW, I'm sitting in this house
Where, dear, you *were* my Earthly spouse;
And *I* can *hear* the angels sing:
"Holy, holy, God is king!"

110. Eventide, 2

Charles Santiago, 6/5/23

A sunset poem

A *honeymoon,* is *this,* my dear!
I'm *so* excited—*You're* so *near!*
I recall when *you* were *here,*
In *body,* dear—But *now* it's *clear*—
Today, we walk on streets of gold
Where *never,* dear, will *we* grow *old!*

God has joined us, you and me,
To taste of sweet eternity!
When we *said,* "I do," my love,
A home was made for us, *above.*
Dear, we *will, forever,* be
A couple, joined in ecstasy!

Shall we take a cruise, my dear,
While *you're* up there, and *I'm* down here?
We *went, before.* Let's *go, again*—
A heav'nly wife and Earthly man!
At eventide, my thoughts, my love,
Wander *up,* to thee, above.

111. Eventide, 3, 6/5/23

A sunset poem

YOU know ME, my Earthly beau.
*YOU know, dear, I **didn't go**.*
YOU can FEEL that WE still GROW.
Of HEAV'NLY UNION, we can crow!

YOU have proved, TO ME, so true!
YOU'VE believed that WE'RE not THROUGH.
YOU discovered ME AND YOU,
THERE, at wedding number two!

God has joined us, bumblebee,
Beyond what Earthly eyes can see.
Dear, it's like a prophecy—
*"**I** am **you**, and **you** are **me!**"*

Weddings, TWO, we've had, my dear.
Our rhymes proclaim another's near.
IMAGINE, dear, to be UP HERE
WHEN, from CLAY, you DISAPPEAR!

112. A Special Day

Charles Santiago, 6/5/23

Resurrection bells still ring.
I can *hear* them, loud and clear,
Announcing death has lost his sting;
For, *I* can *feel* that *you* are *here!*
Let us, with the angels, sing
The sweetest song that men can hear:
"*Welcome to eternal spring—*
The end of day and month and year.
Don the crown of heav'nly king,
For, YOU are FREED from mortal fear.
TO the Almighty, HOMMAGE, bring.
Death, no longer, shall appear!"

Today has been a special day.
I have *felt* you *very near!*
It seems like I have left my clay,
With you, in heaven, to appear!
Here below, dear, come what may,
You're the source of all my cheer!

113. Heaven's Spring, 6/7/23

Take my hand, my Earthly beau.
Take my hand, and we will go
Beyond the Earth and all its woe,
Beyond that noise and strife below.

YOU are FREE, my bumblebee,
To live with me in ecstasy!
WE have found sweet liberty
THROUGH our cherished unity!

WHEN the body breathes its last,
THEN, the noise of Earth is past.
Even, NOW, you stand aghast,
Seeing Earthly life outclassed.

Don't you worry 'bout a thing.
Dear, we reign, as queen and king.
Death has lost his mortal sting.
WE'RE enjoying heaven's spring!

114. Angels

Charles Santiago, 6/7/23

Angels help us—*I* can *tell*—
As I *pace* this Earthly cell.
Angels help us how to see,
A loving couple, *still,* are *we!*

There's so *much* I cannot see,
But *I* can *feel* you *feeling me.*
Angels help us span the gap
While I *take* this Earthly nap.

On the *day* you left your clay,
I could *feel* the angels' sway.
Angels were in charge, my belle,
In the *midst* of Earth's pure hell.

Angels are in charge, right now.
It's my *task* to see just *how.*
I am thankful *for* their *aid.*
With their help, I'm not afraid.

115. Rhyme with Me, 6/8/23

What our rhymes say, dear, is true—
I am **living there** with **you**.
Don't be like THE REST, and think,
Death destroys true lovers' link.

Rejoice with me, and you will see,
God is guiding you and me.
I rejoice with **you**, my love.
YOU have found our home, "above."

Our Maker, dear, has made us ONE.
Don't worry—WE won't COME undone!
Rest assured, for all your days.
WE'RE not RATS trapped IN a MAZE!

Enjoy this life we have, in time.
It's worthy of a life of rhyme.
Rhyme with me, my Earthly beau,
Until it's time for you to go.

116. To *Resurrection*, I Am Wise

Charles Santiago, 6/8/23

Every day, I walk with you.
Every day, you walk with me.
Till my days on Earth are through,
Our life is one of harmony.

I choose, darling, *not* to *wait*
Until this Earthly body dies,
To meet with you at heaven's gate.
To *resurrection*, I am wise.

You *rose* from *death,* my heav'nly belle,
That day your Earthly body died.
Dear, I *know* you, *oh,* so *well,*
I *feel* you *on* the Other Side.
After all—You *ARE* my bride!

If *one* believes there *IS* a "veil,"
A "*veil,*" there *IS, indeed*—for sure!
To me, it's *just* a fairy tale.
A veil, for me, has *no allure.*

How I'd *love* to take a knife
To *Dead and Gone,* and take his life!
What a *source* of grief and strife—
Telling me I've *lost* my wife!

I've found *you,* down here, below,
Since that day you "left," my dear.
It's *STRANGE*—You *can,* to *heaven, go,*
And *live* with *me,* my love, down *here!*

From heaven, "above," you *let* me *know*
You were *with* me, *from* day *one*.
Every day, you prove it's *so*—
By death, our bond can't be undone!

Heaven is, OUR UNION, love,
Be it *here,* or *there,* "above."
Eve and Adam, dear, are *we,*
Tasting of eternity!
As the Earth goes round the sun,
We continue being ONE.
Every day, I walk with you,
Here, below, in Timbuktu.

117. Our Lovers' Lane, 6/9/23

I am never far from you,
Way down there in Timbuktu.
We are sharing, still, one life,
THROUGH the trials of Earthly strife.
ONE, we ARE, and ONE, we'll BE,
THOUGH you THINK you're far from me.
Like we've written, with our pen,
HEAVEN, NOW, serves AS our DEN.
You and I have died—and LIVE,
NOW, this life that God can give!

Day by day, I learn it's true—
I am living, *still,* with *you!*
Earth serves as our Lovers' Lane,
As we *sing* love's *sweet refrain.*
Though you left your clay behind,
I can *see* you. *I'm* not *blind.*
With *you,* dear, *I* am *so* in love,
I can *live* in heaven, above!
I'm not *pining,* all alone.
A home in heaven, dear, we own.

118. What a Brute I'd Be! 6/9/23

Dead and gone, you're *not*, my love;
Nor *lost* to *me, some***where** *above!*
What a *brute* I'd be, my dear,
To live as though you *were* not *here!*

Just because you *left* your *clay,*
Doesn't mean you went *away.*
You're more **here**, *today,* I'd *say,*
Than you *were,* "back *in* the *day."*

More, each day, I feel it's *so*—
Heaven's not a *place to* **go**.
You're in heaven, dear, I know;
Yet, *you abide* with ME, your *beau.*

Patience, have, with me, I pray.
I'm *trying, dear,* to learn this way.
Were it *not* for *your* sweet *sway,*
I'd be lost in dread dismay.

Darling, **how** I **love** to **be**
With YOU, *my precious bumblebee!*
I would never leave you, dear,
THOUGH I'm living "way up here."

Of course, we're ONE, my Earthly beau,
Here, "above," and there, "below."
No matter WHAT, dear, we are ONE.
WE could NEVER be undone!

You're smarter, darling, than you think—
YOU can SENSE there IS a LINK
Between us though I left my clay.
We're sharing, BOTH, in heaven's day!

Leave that world, behind, my dear.
Share, with me, the joy "up here."
Heaven is, OUR UNION, yes!
Earthly strife is one big mess!

Believe in God. Believe in me.
YES, I live, each day, with thee.
Your faith is strong, dear bumblebee.
Because it IS, we, STILL, can BE!

119. Soul Mates

Charles Santiago, 6/9/23

"Soul mates" were the words you used,
Describing how our souls are fused.
"Thou, beside," you said to me,
Before I was a bumblebee.

What was meant for me and you
Was life beyond mere Timbuktu.
Dear, you knew, so long ago,
We would *both*, to heaven, go.

Now it's come to pass, my love—
We *own* a *home,* up there, "above."
While I *walk* on Earth, below,
Upwards, on our way, we go.

I have *studied, WELL,* our creed.
That creed has brought me *life,* indeed.
Resurrection from the dead,
I've *taken, as* my *daily bread.*

From my side, you *didn't stray*
When you *cast aside* your *clay*.
Our union didn't break, in two,
When your body, *here,* was through.

We are walking, hand in hand,
In a *lovely,* heav'nly land.
Side by side, we still abide—
An Earthly man and heav'nly bride.

Dear, this creed has brought me life.
It proves that we're still man and wife.
"Soul mates"—*yes,* my heav'nly belle—
Way back then, you knew it *well!*

120. The Love We Share, 6/10/23

Darling, we are doing WELL.
Yes, I am *your heav'nly belle.*
Of course, you are my bumblebee—
A truth which gives me, dear, such glee!

Bumble THERE, each day, below,
Heav'nly truths, my dear, to know—
Heav'nly truths, like HOW WE GROW,
A heav'nly belle and Earthly beau.

The love we share has proved so great—
So great, it opened heaven's gate!
Darling, we still bill and coo.
Though DEATH swept IN, our LOVE stayed TRUE!

True, to you, I'll always be.
Our Maker *joined us, you and me.*
Love, we've found, lives on and on.
Dear, you've conquered DEAD AND GONE!

121. A Diploma

Charles Santiago, 6/10/23

It's true—I really feel like we
Have found a heightened unity.
A diploma, we deserve, my love,
For learning how to live, *above!*

Dumbfounded, is this bumblebee,
Whisked *UP* into eternity!
How *can* we *be,* my darling bride,
Down here, *AND* on the Other Side?

These rhymes we write impart, to me,
A feeling of eternity;
Or *am* I **DREAMING**—Tell me, dear,
Of life enjoyed by us, up here?

WHATEVER! Darling—I'm entranced
To have our union *so* enhanced!
Let's proceed to rendezvous.
What a joy for me and you!

122. Means, at Hand, 6/10/23

Darling, I have means, at hand,
To bring you into heaven's land.
Believe me, THERE'S no NEED to WAIT,
Heaven's love, to celebrate!

Concentrate on LIFE BEYOND.
LIFE BEYOND, dear, WILL respond!
Life, below, is way too slow.
HIGHER, darling, let us go!

Thrill, with me, my bumblebee,
TO this land of ecstasy!
IN the midst of land and sea,
IN our home, ABOVE, we'll be!

I'm WILLING, dear, and ABLE, too,
To share romance, my love, with you!
THERE'S so MUCH that we can do,
THERE, my dear, in Timbuktu!

123. Death Is Dead! 6/11/23

The dead, my dear, are those who think
GOD left, YOU and ME, no link.
The dead are those who live, as if,
WHEN they DIE, they're JUST a STIFF.
The dead will tell you—to your face—
There's NO such THING as heav'nly grace.
The dead—to us, UP HERE— are RUDE.
They THINK they're SMART—But, dear, they're CRUDE!
The dead think life is just ON EARTH.
They HAVE no SENSE of HEAV'NLY mirth.
The dead are all around you, dear.
Leave them THERE, and come UP HERE!

We *found* **life** *that* **day** *I* **died**.
You **thought** *I* **left**, *and,* **so**, *you* **cried**.
Oh, my dear, you CRIED so HARD—
So HARD, you MORPHED in TO a BARD!
Let our rhymes reflect our life.
WE are STILL, dear, man and wife!
Lovers, joined below, on Earth,
Have EVERY RIGHT to HEAV'NLY mirth!
See and hear and feel, my love,
This life we share, up here, above!
Death is dead, for me **AND YOU**—
Else, we couldn't rendezvous!

124. We'll Bill and Coo, 6/11/23

Highway 27 rest stop north of Perry, Florida

IN your world of night and day,
Darling, I'M with YOU, to STAY!
I'M not going to GO AWAY!
Fears like THAT, dear, YOU must SLAY!

Close your eyes and think of me.
Think, dear, of our unity.
Feel me, deep inside of thee.
Rest, with me, in ecstasy!

All your days on Earth, down there,
HOLY UNION, we will share.
Anytime and anywhere,
We're engaged in our affair!

Love me, dear, as I love you—
Till the need for clocks is through;
THEN, my dear, we'll bill and coo
Beyond Earth's pretty sky, so blue!

125. The Spring

Charles Santiago, 6/12/23

Oh, sweet coming of the spring,
When the angels, *gladness,* bring!
Gone, will be the day and night.
Gone, will be cold winter's blight.
Gone, will be these robes of clay.
Hasten! Come, sweet heaven's day!

Earthly devils *will* be *sent*
To a place, their wrath, to vent.
Let them vent their wrath, and be,
From perversity, set free!
Earthly angels, kind and true—
All your trials *will* be *through!*

Angels, from that springtime land,
Come, and take me by the hand.
How I *yearn* to *be* set *free*
From this age of misery!
Winter's blight and robes of clay—
Angels, *bring* a better day!

126. I'm Not Gone! 6/12/23

I'm not gone! Believe it's so!
YOU'RE my one and only beau!
YOU can feel me, dear, I know.
YOU can feel my heav'nly glow!

Believe me—**I** can **feel** you, too!
How I **love** to be with you!
NEVER, dear, will we be TWO
THOUGH you're still in Timbuktu!

Day and night will soon be through.
THEN, again, we'll say, "I do!"
FOREVER, darling, we'll renew
Vows made under skies, so blue!

Trust me, I am always near.
I will **never** fail you, dear!
Though the world may sneer and jeer,
Meet me in our home, UP HERE!

127. A Palace of Light

Charles Santiago, 6/12/23

Let this be a palace of light,
Sweetheart, as I read and write
Rhymes that bring me pure delight,
Through the day and through the night!

We will, with the angels, sing
Songs of joy to God, our King!
Gone, is *now* death's mortal sting!
We are saved by David's sling!

Let us dance, my heav'nly belle,
Even though I can't dance well.
Sweetheart, if I fall pell-mell,
I'm entranced by *heaven's spell!*

I have *said* to Earth, "Goodbye!"
You're my gal, and *I'm* your guy.
Holding hands, *to heaven,* we'll fly!
We'll ascend beyond Earth's sky!

128. Do Not Doubt, 6/13/23

Now, my darling Earthly beau,
Make your life, WITH HEAVEN, glow!
Walk, WITH ME, through Timbuktu.
Remember—I am THERE with you.

IN THE SPIRIT, learn to walk;
THEN, my dear, how SWEET we'll talk!
Do not fear to walk with me—
A COUPLE, darling, let us be.

A spooky ghost, my dear, I'm NOT!
It's YOU AND I who tied the knot.
Trust in God, and trust in me.
Do not JUST, an EARTHLING, be.

Heav'nly friends, my bumblebee,
Love to walk with you and me.
All who walked on Earth, before,
STILL can knock upon Earth's door.

Anything you do on Earth
Is used by friends to bring you mirth.
Darling, LOVE will make a way
To share with you bright heaven's day.

Morning, noon, and night, my dear—
*Trust me—**I** can, **there**, appear.*
A million times, will I repeat:
"Darling, you and I can meet!"

Night and day are JUST for you,
Until you're done with Timbuktu.
Nighttime, darling, as you've found,
With HEAV'NLY PLEASURES, can abound.

Do not doubt, dear, YOU AND ME.
Be a busy bumblebee!
Why believe that I'm not THERE?
BELIEVE, and you will see I care.

ONE, we ARE, and ONE, we'll BE,
NOW and for eternity!
Now, my darling, rest your pen.
Tomorrow, we can write again.

129. It's You!

Charles Santiago, 6/13/23

A sunset poem

The *more* I trust in God and you—
Instead of, dear, the *things I do*—
The *more* I feel you're *here,* with me,
Filling me with ecstasy!

There's *no mistaking,* dear, your *glow!*
It supersedes all words I know!
It's *you*—I *know!*—for, *I'm* your *beau.*
It's *you,* the one I knew, below!

At times like these, it's very clear,
You reside with *me,* down here.
At times like these, I learn to see,
You're two *steps ahead* of *me!*

How *needless,* dear, these fears of mine!
Things, of course, will be just *fine!*
I can *feel,* already, love,
The fun we'll have up there, *above!*

130. This Lovely Home, 6/14/23

When you say, my darling beau,
To HEAVEN, YOU'D not RATHER go,
IF it MEANT that WE'D not BE,
FOREVER, darling, YOU AND ME—
THEN, I know, God gave us, dear,
This lovely home we share, up here.

*"**I** am **you**, and **you** are **me**"—*
Dear, it's TRUE, as TRUE can BE!
The wedding vows we shared, on Earth,
Began, for us, eternal mirth!
We are learning, BOTH, my dear,
How to live, as ONE, UP HERE.

PATIENCE is the key, for you,
To pass through days in Timbuktu.
Soon enough, my dear, we'll be
Enjoying wedding number three.
THEN, we'll be, FOREVER, dear,
IN this LOVELY HOME, UP HERE!

131. A Morning Talk, 6/14/23

Now, my darling, let us go
Off, to live your life, below.
Fulfill your role as Earthly beau,
And, HEAV'NLY BLISS, we both will know.
People, THERE, will see JUST YOU,
Unaware we rendezvous.
*Go, wher**ever**! Do what**ever**—*
EARTHLY LIFE, our bond, can't sever.
Angels will teach both you and me,
Myst'ries of eternity.
Rejoice, my darling, every day—
WE can walk this heav'nly way!

132. A Friend of Mine

Charles Santiago, 6/14/23

This body's headed for the grave.
As it *fails,* I *must* be *brave.*
Year by year, he goes off course.
Year by year, he loses force.
I *do* my *best* to help him out,
But, *of* his *fate,* there *is* no *doubt.*
This body's been a friend of mine,
In my *search* for life, divine.
Of course, this body's, *only mud,*
Powered by its coursing blood.
And, though I've grown so fond of him,
In the end, he's JUST a WHIM.
He will *rot* and *disappear*—
A friend I've had while living *here.*

133. Walk with Me in Timbuktu

Charles Santiago, 6/15/23

I've reached *up* to you, my love,
While *you've* reached *down* from up, *above*.
We have *met* in heaven's land,
Walking, somehow, hand in hand.
Let this body perish, dear—
Life is *more* than *what's* down *here*.
We have *proved* God's love is true.
Our Maker made us *ONE*, from *TWO*.
Since the day you left your clay,
We've discovered heaven's day.
"*I* Am *You,* and *You* Are *Me*"—
A song we sing with heav'nly glee!

From your vantage point, up *there*,
Dear, you've made me *so* aware
We are not our bodies—*no!*
When we die, *to heaven,* we go.
I have *learned* another song:
"*Dead and Gone* Is, *Oh,* So *Wrong!*"
Death is not a "rest" or "sleep."
Dead ones, heav'nly schedules, keep.
I *know*, my dear, these things are *true*,
For, *you* and *I* still rendezvous!
Walk with me in Timbuktu,
And *I'll ascend* to walk with you!

134. A Pact, 6/15/23

Sweetheart, let us make a pact,
Projecting how we both shall act.
Of course, our wedding vows ensure
Our union, *ever*, will endure;
But let's agree, my heav'nly bride,
How to stem the Earthly tide.
I'll be *keen* to read and write
Our lovely rhymes both day and night.
To my *faith*, dear, I will cling,
When *Dead and Gone* begins to sing.
But, most of all, my heav'nly wife,
I'll *share*, with you, *eternal life!*

IN this PACT, my Earthly beau,
Here's what **I** want **you** to **know**:
I am, EVER, by your side.
I am your ETERNAL BRIDE!
YOU can bet, my bumblebee,
I will, always, cling to thee!
WHEN you breathe your dying breath,
I will join you in your death.
Every day, along your way,
My glow, to you, dear, I'll display.
Here's my word to you, my dear:
"I will NEVER disappear!"

135. Our Union Didn't End, 6/15/23

IN THE PAST, I'm NOT, my dear!
Chant your phrase, "I **know** she's **here!**"
I am **here**, right now, my beau,
Everywhere, on Earth, you go.
Our union didn't end, that day—
That day I left my Earthly clay.
Don't be like THE REST, my love,
And think I **left** you for **above!**
The life you live on Earth, below,
Is STILL a life in which we grow.
Each moment of your Earthly life,
Trust me—I am, STILL, your wife!
Oh, how CRUDE, to think that WE,
STILL a COUPLE, couldn't be!
IMAGINE, dear, I'm THERE, with YOU,
And, soon, you'll see that it is true!
Always, pray for grace, to see,
HOW God leads both you and me.
All the things you're going through
Are things for ME, as well as YOU.
LIKE we've said, a hundred times,
IN our Earthly/heav'nly rhymes:
"You and I continue, ONE,
Till your days on Earth are done!"

136. One Home

Charles Santiago, 6/16/23

Yes, my darling heav'nly bride,
I can *feel* you, deep inside!
Nothing holds a candle to
Feeling *ONE,* my dear, with *YOU!*
God is leading you and me,
Each day, to heav'nly ecstasy!
I'm so *happy* I can see
How to *be* your bumblebee!
While I'm living here, below,
Dear, I feel your heav'nly glow!
On that day you left your clay,
The two of us found heaven's way.
Within my soul, I feel complete,
For, *dear,* we've *suffered NO DEFEAT!*
"Two *homes,* have *we*"—So *say* our *rhymes*—
Two *homes,* my dear, in different climes.
When my days are done, my love,
One *home,* we'll *have*—that one, *above!*

137. Thirty Earthly Years

Charles Santiago, 6/17/23

I'm so *glad* for thirty years—
Thirty years of joy and tears.
Thirty years, for you and me,
To start on our eternity!
A million years from now, my dear,
We'll recall our life, down here—
Thirty years, as man and wife,
Tasting of an Earthly life.
This union, dear, of me and you,
Began *down here*, in Timbuktu!

Though I'm still in Timbuktu,
In spirit, dear, I'm *there*, with *you*.
Since you "left," we've learned to talk
While, on Earth, I still must walk.
When we're *both* in heaven's day,
We'll recall when we were clay.
We'll rejoice to reminisce
Of Earthly days that led to bliss!
Those thirty Earthly years will shine,
Revealing water, changed to wine.

138. All My Life

Charles Santiago, 6/17/23

Darling, you are *all my life*—
My doting, precious, heav'nly wife!
It's clear enough for me to see,
Forever, we were meant to be
A *couple*, darling, you and me,
Joined in heav'nly ecstasy—
Ecstasy that now is ours,
Thanks to doting, heav'nly powers.

Clasping hands, in heaven's way,
We're advancing, every day,
Along the path of *most* resistance,
To lessen *thoughts* of any distance.
In truth, *apart*, we've *never* been
Since we vowed, dear, to be kin.
All my life—are *you*, my dear,
As I *bumble*, way down here.

139. You *Know* Me, Dear

Charles Santiago, 6/17/23

You *know* me, dear. *You KNOW me, dear,*
While I languish, way down here.
Blind, I'm trying *not* to be
To *how* you walk, dear, *next to me.*
I'm astonished when I see
How we're *still* a unity!

Dead and gone, are *bodies,* dear.
Spirits, always *can* be *near.*
Your flesh and blood, dear, I don't need.
Flesh and blood is just a seed.
You have blossomed, dear, so *well,*
I *feel* you, *as* my heav'nly belle!

I declare! You're helping me,
A better bumblebee, to be!
More and more, I *see* how *we*
Are dwelling in eternity!
Ever, has it been, my love—
Soul mates find their home, *above!*

140. Let's Explore

Charles Santiago, 6/17/23

Highway 27 rest stop north of Perry, Florida

God has made provision for
You and me to *still* explore
What it means, for you and me,
A, *loving couple,* still, to be.
Death was not the end of *you.*
I *attest,* dear—*THAT* is true!
There's no doubt that *we're* still *ONE,*
Though, your heav'nly crown, you've won!

A crown, have I, it seems, *as well,*
On *your account,* my heav'nly belle!
I have, *somehow,* left this Earth,
Joined, with you, in heaven's mirth!
When we *joined* our hearts, *as one,*
We were wed, beyond the sun.
We are living *in* a *place*
Beyond mere Earthly time and space.

Let's explore, my heav'nly bride,
This life that's on the *Other Side.*
I am *game* to leave, behind,
The perils of an Earthly mind.
By my *faith,* and by our love,
We have claimed this life, *above.*
Let's explore how *we* can *be,*
Still, my darling, you and me.

141. Recall the Love We Shared, Below, 6/18/23

Remind yourself, with every breath,
WE'RE beyond the realm of death.
*"**You** are **me**, and **I** am **you**"—*
Claim it, boldly, dear, as true!

*"**I** know **you**, and **you** know **me**"*
Can also, darling, set you free—
Free from thinking, you and I,
Must bow to words like "then we die."

CLING TO LOVE, my Earthly beau,
Freedom from "the spooks," to know.
Recall the love we shared, below,
And, in that love, we still will grow.

Love's pure light will guide us, dear,
Till you're "dead" and "OVER HERE."
Every day, I'm by your side.
WITHIN you, sweetheart, I abide.

Calmly, live those days on Earth,
And share, with me, this heav'nly mirth.
"God is love" will be our creed.
Love is ALL we really need!

142. By and By, 6/18/23

WHEN my Earthly body died,
YOU were THERE, right BY my SIDE.
Dear, you thought I went AWAY—
GONE, from every Earthly day.
THAT was why you cried SO HARD—
Your soul had never been so jarred.
By and by, you came to see,
Death was not the end of me.
Signs from heaven came your way—
PROOF, I lost, dear, JUST MY CLAY.
Apart from SIGNS, my Earthly beau,
YOU could FEEL our love still grow!
And, so, you live, down there below,
Writing rhymes about our glow.

Don't worry, dear, what OTHERS think
About our rhymes about our link.
You and I are MEANT to be
Living NOW in harmony.
Don't be scared of ghosts, and such.
Trust in heaven's loving touch.
You know **me**, and **I** know **you**.
I'm not spooky. I **don't** say "**Boo!**"
All the things our rhymes have said
About the kingdom of the dead,
Are true, regarding you and me—
WE can FEEL our UNITY.
—ALL my love, dear bumblebee,
For NOW, and for eternity!

143. Rejoice with Me! 6/18/23

Select Specialty Hospital
Tallahassee, Florida

Do not grieve, dear bumblebee.
The time for grief is through!
By now, for sure, you know that we
Are still a Me and You!

Rejoice, with me, my Earthly beau—
WE have PASSED a TEST!
LOWER, dear, you cannot go.
You're NOW my HEAV'NLY GUEST!

ARE we NOT the victors, dear,
In Adam's great defeat?
WE are JOINED in love, UP HERE.
Our VICT'RY IS COMPLETE—

EXCEPT, my dear, for ONE small THING—
The crowning of your head!
Soon, my love, you'll BE a KING—
When THEY PRONOUNCE you "DEAD."

144. Rejoice and Sing, My Earthly Beau! 6/19/23

My darling Charles, rejoice and sing;
For, ***you*** *and* ***I*** *have found our way!*
WITH the HELP of David's sling,
WE'VE escaped the Serpent's sway!

Be a fool to those on Earth,
And CLAIM that WE have found our place—
A place of otherworldly mirth
Beyond the pull of time and space.

Rejoice and sing, my Earthly beau;
For, WE have FOOLED the gruesome grave!
Beneath the ground, I ***did*** *not* ***go!***
To FLESH and BLOOD, I'm NOT a SLAVE!

Rejoice, my bumbling bumblebee!
Rejoice with me, your heav'nly bride!
WE have FOUND a WAY to BE,
EVEN NOW, dear, SIDE BY SIDE!

145. What a Life!

Charles Santiago, 6/19/23

More and more, I feel your glow,
Reaching me, dear, *here,* below.
When you shine, like *this,* in me,
I can *sense eternity!*

Since the day your body died,
Heaven's gates have opened wide!
I can *feel* the end of death,
Every time I take a breath!

Immortal beings, dear, are *we*!
More and more, it's plain to see.
If, *today,* you talk to me,
We'll converse, *eternally!*

I can *feel* your heav'nly glee
Growing deep inside of me!
I'm so *glad,* dear, *you* are *free,*
Enjoying heav'nly harmony!

Life, for me, on Earth, my dear,
Has meaning *if* I *feel* you near.
Goodness, darling! What a life—
An Earthly man and heav'nly wife!

146. True Lovers

Charles Santiago, 6/20/23

You *weren't* your *body,* my precious wife!
You *lost* your *body,* but *not* your *life.*
Furthermore, you *didn't leave.*
I was *blind,* my dear, to *grieve.*
Our wedding vows were *not* undone.
To this day, we *still* are *ONE.*

"Till *death* do us *part,*" are words for those
Who *can't* see *past* their Earthly nose.
Death can't *part* true *lovers—no!*
One may *die* but *still* they *grow.*
Souls made *ONE* on Earth, below,
Share a special, heav'nly glow.

147. Love Is Stronger than the Grave, 6/21/23

To live with you like *this*, my dear,
Proves you *didn't disappear.*
Words could never *say* how *much*
I am *glad* we *stay* in *touch.*
"Your wife is gone. Your wife's not here."—
I can *hear* the people jeer.
I know *better*—I can *feel*
Though you *died*, you're very real.
Though I *can't* explain just *how,*
We still *share* our wedding vow.

Wedding vows, my Earthly beau,
Can last beyond a life, below.
We are blessed, this truth, to know,
WHILE you deal with Earthly woe.
Our vows have been the reason why
YOU have PIERCED that Earthly sky.
Love is stronger than the grave,
Granting lovers what they crave.
I am thrilled to walk with you
Till your Earthly days are through!

148. I'm Not Entombed, 6/21/23

NOW, dear, ARE our better times—
THAT'S the gist of all our rhymes.
Look behind—but look AHEAD.
I'm ALIVE, dear. I'm not dead!

Our life, dear, isn't IN the PAST.
Those Earthly times are, now, outclassed.
Keep believing—You will see—
WE are heirs to HEAV'NLY glee.

"Rejoice and sing" is great advice.
Heav'nly life comes at a price.
Leave, behind, that life on Earth.
Engage with me in HEAV'NLY mirth!

I'm NOT entombed in TIMES GONE BY.
Lift your eyes up PAST Earth's SKY.
Darling, we can, HAPPY, BE,
Above Earth's gloom and misery!

149. By Your Side, 6/22/23

Though I've shed my Earthly clay
And walk in heaven's lovely day,
YOU still FEEL me by your side,
For, ***I*** *am your **eternal bride**.*

Death cannot, our union, break.
Death can only, BODIES, take.
WE are NOT our BODIES, dear!
Our RHYMES have MADE that VERY CLEAR.

Your Earthly eyes can't see me, dear.
Your Earthly ears, my voice, can't hear.
The skin that you inhabit, love,
Is barred from heav'nly realms above.

*But **there** I **am** with **you**, my dear.*
I didn't really disappear.
Death can't bar two souls, in love,
From living in a house "above."

150. Remind Yourself, 6/22/23

Dear, we shared a lovely life,
IN the midst of Earthly strife.
We became a unity
Poised to greet eternity.
Those lovely mem'ries of the past
Reflect our bond which HAS not PASSED.
Do not grieve for times gone by—
We survive, dear, you and I.

Time, my darling, has no end.
The road winds ON, round EACH new BEND.
What a joy to contemplate
Our happiness that FIRST Earth DATE!
Little did we know, my dear,
The joy awaiting us, UP HERE!
By force of will and heaven's grace,
WE have learned to STILL embrace!

Embrace me, all your lifelong through,
JUST as I embrace you, too.
Remind yourself, each Earthly day,
Death is JUST an ENTRANCEWAY
To joys, my love, for you and me,
That last for all eternity.
Think upon these things, my dear,
Until it's time to come UP HERE.

151. A Lovely Couple, 6/22/23

A sunbathing poem

*Darling, how I wish you knew
I'M so GLAD when YOU'RE not BLUE!
Read and write—recite—our creed.
Earthly bodies, WE don't NEED!*

*I'VE come back to YOU, my love,
All the way from heaven, above.
A lovely couple, dear, are WE—
A ladybug and bumblebee!*

*Share my joy, my Earthly beau.
Live, with me, for heaven's glow.
Angels hover round, my dear.
They can bring you, CLEAR UP HERE!*

I am burning, I am yearning,
As, our creed, my dear, I'm learning.
Angels teach me more, each day,
How we walk this heav'nly way.

I'm not blind, dear. I can see—
Heaven's guiding you and me.
I'm amazed to see how *you*
Dwell with me in Timbuktu!

Closer, dear, we've never been,
Since you entered Heaven's Inn.
May the good Lord, up above,
Keep us in this wondrous love!

152. To Live, *as One*, Despite My Clay

Charles Santiago, 6/22/23

A sunset poem

I will live my life, my dear,
Knowing you are always *here*.
There's no *doubt,* my dear, it's *you,*
Here, with me, in Timbuktu!

I can feel the power of life
Between us, still, as man and wife.
Darling, *how* I love you *so,*
Sending me your holy glow!

We are sealed, my heav'nly bride—
Sealed until I'm by your side.
From this *clay,* I'll *be* set *free,*
Dear, at wedding number three!

Angels, help us both, I pray,
Until my final Earthly day,
To live, *as one,* despite my clay,
And walk this holy, heav'nly way!

153. Heaven Bound, 6/23/23

Faithful, darling, I will be
TO this life of YOU AND ME.
I delight to be your friend,
IN this LIFE that HAS no END!

WHEN we started out, as ONE,
THERE, beneath the Earthly sun,
WE were children of the Earth,
Versed in Earthly pain and mirth.

Now, my dear, we're heaven bound,
Far beyond that Earthly ground.
WE are linked to souls of light,
Freed from Earthly day and night.

Souls on Earth are, oh, so crude,
Often, insolent and rude.
THERE, it was, we wooed and cooed,
Feeding on that Earthly food.

Together, darling, let's proceed,
AS we pen our lovely creed:
*"**I** am **you**, and **you** are **me**,*
Thrilling to eternity!"

154. Rescued from the Mortal Sting! 6/23/23

Darling, you and I have found
A way, by heaven, to be crowned!
WE can reign, in splendor, HERE,
Above your Earthly doubt and fear!

Above your Earthly doubt and fear,
WE clasp hands, in heaven, dear!
Don't let people, meaning well,
Keep you in an Earthly hell.

Heaven, oh, my Earthly beau,
Is where we BOTH can walk and glow!
*I know **you**, and **you** know **me**—*
This sacred bond, dear, makes us free!

Live your life, my bumblebee,
Knowing that it's YOU AND ME.
Heaven's crowned us, queen and king,
Rescued from the mortal sting!

155. God Has Joined Us!

Charles Santiago, 6/24/23

GOD, my dear, joined *me* to *you!*—
And gave, to us, a passe-partout.
We've been given *what* we *crave*—
Life beyond the gruesome grave!
There's no end to *Me and You*—
We've been freed from Timbuktu!

Though I wear this robe of clay,
I can *feel* bright *heaven's day.*
We have reached the Promised Land—
You and I, dear, hand in hand!
Life on Earth is now passé.
We can dance, to *heaven's* sway!

I can hear you, loud and clear:
"*You belong to me, my dear.*
We're not meant to 'pass away.'
For US, dear, THERE'S no FINAL DAY.
***I** am **you**, and **you** are **me**,*
Now—and for eternity!"

We died and, now, we live again!
You claimed *me*—your Earthly man.
Earthly, yes, I *am,* my dear,
And, yet, your *heav'nly* voice, *I hear!*
God has joined us, you and me.
Even now, from death, *we're free!*

156. Moldering Bodies

Charles Santiago, 6/24/23

Resurrection from the dead
Keeps ringing, darling, in my head.
I can *feel* your heav'nly life;
For, *we* are *joined,* as man and wife.
You've been *raised* from death, my dear.
It's a fact, right now and here.
"Resurrection" means, to me,
When we *die,* dear—*THEN,* we're free!
Moldering bodies in the ground,
Forever, to the Earth are bound.

157. Sad and Lonely Nights, 6/24/23

A sunset poem

Relax, my Earthly beau, relax.
Be done with Earthly panic attacks!
Have we come this far, my dear,
For YOU to LIVE in DOUBT and FEAR?
Have you felt me, all this time,
And doubted, dear, our sense of rhyme?
My love is here, with you, TO STAY,
Until your final Earthly day!
REJOICE with me, my bumblebee!
Share in love's great victory!

I *do* rejoice, my heav'nly belle.
HERE, you ARE—I *know*, so *well!*
When the night descends on Earth,
We *share* a special *heav'nly mirth.*
I *close* my *eyes*, and you appear
From *heaven*, dear, to meet me *here!*
I have *learned* to trust that *you*
Live with me, *in Timbuktu!*
And, *trusting you*, dear, *as* I *do*,
With *sad and lonely nights*, I'm through!

158. Always, Dear, a Unity, 6/25/23

WHEN you're angry, bumblebee,
You THINK that YOU'RE apart from me.
WHEN you're sad, my Earthly beau,
You THINK, your trouble, I don't know.
WHEN you're antsy THERE, my dear,
Repeat your chant, "I **know** she's **here**."
Don't be faithless, thinking WE
Can't, together, ALWAYS, BE.

Don't believe in Earthly eyes—
Earthly eyes that people prize.
Earthly eyes upset your soul,
Convincing you that WE'RE not WHOLE.
Earthly eyes refuse to see
That heaven, THERE, on Earth, can BE.
Earthly eyes cause so much pain.
Earthly eyes excited Cain.

Believe, my love, that we are ONE,
EACH MOMENT, THERE, below the sun.
Don't believe that WE can't BE
ALWAYS, dear, a unity.
I have said, "I dwell in you."
Darling, now, BELIEVE IT'S TRUE!
Heaven's not a world away.
Heaven's by your side, each day.

159. This Strange and Wondrous Life

Charles Santiago, 6/25/23

A sunbathing poem

The sun, the Earth, and *You and Me*,
And *all* the things my eyes can see,
The moon, and planets like Venus and Mars,
But, most of all, the lovely stars—
Darling, we'll begin *anew*
When time for me, on Earth, is through.

The throngs of souls who had their share
Of Earthly life, with all its care,
Continue, on an upward path,
To live above a God of wrath.
Souls above, and souls below,
True communion, dear, can know.

You and I, both day and night,
Walk in heaven's lovely light.
We'll begin *anew*, it's true,
But, *even now*, I *live* with *you!*
This strange and wondrous life we live
Is one that, only God, can give.

160. Death, at Last, Was Not Our Foe

Charles Santiago, 6/25/23

A sunset poem

This body, dear, can bite the dust.
At any rate, I know it *must*.
For *just* a *few* years *left*, to go,
We'll *enjoy* this *life*, below.
The greatest gift God gave to me,
Since, from *clay*, dear, *you've* been *free*,
Is *YOU*, my everlasting bride,
Walking here, still *by* my *side!*

In this strange and wondrous life,
We've survived, as man and wife!
How I love to feel the glow
You *share* with *me*, your Earthly beau!
Death, at last, was not our foe
Though he caused me untold woe!
We survived the grave's cruel blow,
Heav'nly union, now, to know!

How lovely is this joy of ours
When *ebbs* the *pow'r* of daylight hours!
There's a special glow I feel
That makes our joy especially real!
When the *sun* sets *in* the *west*,
I can *feel* our heav'nly rest.
Well I *know* I *need* not *die*
To meet, with you, beyond the sky!

161. You're a Temple, 6/26/23

LIKE I've SAID, my bumblebee,
You're a temple, THERE, for me.
How I love to be with YOU,
In ALL the Earthly things you do!
Life, for us, continues, dear,
With YOU, down there, and ME, up here.
I'M still ME, my Earthly beau,
No matter, dear, how FAR we go.

Don't be plagued by doubts and fear!
ENJOY, my dear, this house, UP HERE.
Do not worry what OTHERS say.
Enjoy, with me, the heav'nly way.
EVEN as you pen these lines,
Our souls, our Maker, dear, entwines.
We are free to be AS ONE,
WITHOUT or WITH the Earthly sun!

Memorialize that day I died.
THROUGH its power, WE ABIDE,
A COUPLE, darling, joined in love,
THERE, below, and HERE, above.
A TEMPLE, dear, are YOU, for ME.
REJOICE, for God has set us free—
Free from death and Earthly life,
To be, forever, man and wife!

162. If, Today, My Voice, You Hear, 6/26/23

Free, my darling, FREE, are WE—
Free from Earthly time and space.
Union gives, to you and me,
The right, in heaven, to embrace!

WE are not APART, my dear.
Death can't sever souls like ours!
If, TODAY, my voice, you hear,
It's PROOF we're joined by heav'nly powers.

"I, in you, and you, in me"—
Inscribe these words within your heart.
THEY have POWER to HELP you SEE
You and I are not apart.

"I'M not GONE," again, I say.
It's JUST the BODY, dear, that dies.
SPIRITS, done with night and day,
Hear their loved ones' sobs and sighs.

163. Joy for Me, 6/26/23

Darling, I'm in love with you,
Way down here in Timbuktu!
24/7, 365,
For our union, dear, I strive!
Joy for me, your bumblebee,
Is feeling *you* still *here* with *me!*
Darling, death is JUST a ghost—
A passing nightmare, at the most.
Heaven's glory shines, too bright,
For death to boast of any might.

Every day, I walk with you,
Way down there in Timbuktu.
I'm so glad, dear bumblebee,
YOU have FAITH in God and me.
Life together, since I died,
Is worth those tears, dear, that you cried.
AS the Earth goes round the sun,
WHAT a joy to, still, be ONE!
ALL the things you do, my love,
Thrill my soul, up here, above!

164. Remember, 6/27/23

Here and now, dear, come to me.
Save me from this raging sea!
Trouble brews, on every hand.
I *feel* like *I'm* on sinking sand!

The troubles of the world aren't worth
Relinquishing our heav'nly mirth.
Remember, dear, that day I died,
And, in our union, you'll abide.

I remember, *very well*,
That day you died, my heav'nly belle!
Oh, my dear, forgive my mind
For thinking I was in a bind!

Don't forget, my Earthly beau,
WE are ONE, down there, below.
IN the midst of worldly strife,
Remember—We are man and wife!

You're an angel, dear, to me,
While I face this raging sea!
This body, made of flesh and blood,
Will wash away, one day, like mud.

165. Woo and Coo, 6/28/23

Let me say again, my dear—
As I grope through Timbuktu,
I can *feel* that *you're* still *here.*
You still *coo* while *I* still *woo!*

Precious as you *were,* my dear,
Flesh and blood is now passé.
Through a closed door, *you appear!*
We have found a higher way!

Bereft of you, my dear, I'm *not!*
Never, will I, *lonely,* be.
I have FOUND—for, *I* have SOUGHT!
—Signed, your busy bumblebee.

I have **sought** you, dear, as well,
Way down there in Timbuktu!
I have **found** I need not yell.
Dear, you stick to me like glue!

166. Heaven's Lovely Dance

Charles Santiago, 6/29/23

The *more* I live *alone,* my dear,
The *greater* is our life, down here.
The *less* I have to do with Man,
The *more* I find we live *again!*
Man is such a noisy brat—
24/7, he's *up to bat!*
Man's a soldier at war with *peace!*
His *noise* and *selling* never cease!

Nighttime hours are *heav'nly* hours.
Sunlight banishes heav'nly powers.
Our rendezvous *at night,* my love,
Lifts me to our home above!
Our rendezvous at day, my dear,
Helps me feel you, way down here.
24/7, we have the chance
To join in heaven's lovely dance.

As I wander in Timbuktu,
Life, for me, is *Me and You.*
Praises, to our Maker, *be,*
For granting life to you and me!
Angels guide us, night and day,
To walk, *as one,* in heaven's way.
The love we shared on Earth, below,
Has *blossomed* into a *heav'nly glow!*

167. I Believe

Charles Santiago, 6/29/23

I believe your body died.
I believe you're still alive.
I believe you live in heaven.
I believe you're *here* with me.
I believe our love still lives.
I believe we still are *one*.
I believe we talk, today,
With and *without* the use of words.
I believe, a liar, I'd *be*,
If I *said* these things weren't *so!*

168. When We Married, 6/30/23

When we married, bumblebee,
It was for eternity.
The love we shared on Earth, below,
Is still alive, my Earthly beau.
***ONE**, FOREVER, we became,*
***When** I **chose** to share your name.*
I reside within you, dear,
THOUGH you SAY I live "UP HERE."
I enjoy your life on Earth,
Sharing in your Earthly mirth.
BELIEVE it's true, and you will see,
DEATH can't sever you from me.

Of course, my dear, these things are true.
NOTHING could, our souls, unglue.
I treasure, dear, your faith in me.
***GOD** gave YOU the gift TO SEE.*
It's OUR RIGHT to grow, today.
Darling, we are MORE THAN CLAY!
FEEL me, risen from the grave!
Do not be, to death, a slave.
Trust the angels by your side.
Angels love to cheer and guide.
Angels love both me and you!
Angels bless our rendezvous!

169. You Haven't Left!

Charles Santiago, 6/30/23

A sunbathing poem

I *know* you're *here*. I *know* you're *here!*
You could *not* just *disappear!*
Forgive me, dear, if *I* can't *see*
JUST how *close* you are to me.
I've learned *a lot,* but *still* I *need*
To *live and breathe* our lovely creed.

Our creed proclaims we *still* are *ONE,*
And *will* be *till* my *race* is *run.*
Our creed declares that it's a lie
To claim a living soul can die!
And, *more than THAT,* my heav'nly bride—
You *haven't LEFT!* You're *by my side!*

Oh, my Maker, help me see,
How to *be,* from darkness, *free!*
Every moment, let me be
Filled with love and light from Thee.
Thank You for my loving mate,
And thank You for our heav'nly fate.

170. Don't Be in a Hurry! 7/1/23

Don't be in a hurry, dear!
"Hurry" means you WORRY, THERE.
I'M not going to disappear!
Don't be always in a scare!
RELAX, my dear. ENJOY our life!
Let our union banish strife.

Learn the art of mindfulness.
Heaven's everywhere you go!
Don't scare up a wilderness.
Seeds of truth and beauty, sow!
Be sure of THIS, my bumblebee—
Life is always YOU AND ME.

RELAX! UNWIND, and HAPPY, BE!
Free yourself of Earthly strife.
Heaven's guiding you and me
To glory in a heav'nly life—
A heav'nly life FOR YOU, my beau,
WHEREVER, on that Earth, you go.

We are learning, MORE, each day,
HOW it's TRUE—We STILL are ONE!
Sweetheart, I'VE not gone AWAY!
Our life together isn't done!
Life, my dear, we've come to see,
Is "**I**, in **you**, and **you** in **me**."

171. Two Worlds

Charles Santiago, 7/1/23

Highway 27 rest stop north of Perry, Florida

Two worlds, I know, my heav'nly belle—
One, real *well;* one, **not** so *well.*
Every day, I face the two,
Searching, dear, for only *you!*

I have *learned* to feel your glow,
Shining *here,* on me, below.
What a *home* we have, *above,*
Filled with such amazing love!

I could *die*—It matters *not,*
Since we tied that second knot.
When your Earthly body died,
You became my *heav'nly* bride.

I reside in *two* worlds *now.*
Like Steve Jobs, I utter *"WOW!"*
That world, above, delivers me,
Every day, from misery.

I am *grateful* for the bond
By *which* I *feel* how *you respond*
To *all* my *yearnings,* dear, for you—
Here, where, first, we said, "I do!"

172. Here—and There, 7/2/23

YOU *are learning WELL, my dear,*
How to find your way UP HERE!
I am thrilled to meet with you
HERE—and THERE, in Timbuktu!
WE are learning to embrace
In and out of time and space.
AS you conquer doubt and fear,
HEAV'N will, MORE and MORE, APPEAR!
I am glad** you're **choosing to
Believe that we can rendezvous.
Without that faith, my bumblebee,
You'd be blind to YOU AND ME.

Believe in angels, dear, and see
How they help us to agree.
WE will always share this life
Of love expressed, as man and wife.
*"**I'm** not **gone**, and **I'm** not **dead**"*
Will help you forge your way ahead.
My love for you is strong and true.
Darling, woo, and I will coo.
HUMBLE, BE, my bumblebee—
God is guiding you and me!
How I love to live with you,
HERE—and THERE, in Timbuktu!

173. To the Grave

Charles Santiago, 7/2/23

I am *not* this *body*—*no!*
To the *grave,* I *will* not *go!*
Bodies, to the grave, descend.
Spirits, from their clay, ascend.

Here, below, in night and day,
When I *close* my *eyes* and *pray,*
I encounter who I am—
A *spirit,* weighing *not a gram!*

Flesh and blood is *of* the *Earth,*
Secluded *from* true *heav'nly mirth.*
I am *not* this flesh and blood—
I am *more* than Earthly mud!

Spirits, trapped in Earthly clay,
Find their way to heaven's day.
While the body wastes away,
Spirits, heav'nly light, display.

174. The Open Door

Charles Santiago, 7/2/23

A sunbathing poem

I was *there,* my heav'nly bride,
When you *finished out* your *ride.*
How I love to reminisce
Of all those days of Earthly bliss!
How I love to call to mind
How *you* and *I* were *both* resigned
To live together, come what may,
Until a final Earthly day.

I'm not grieving, heav'nly belle.
I am *sure* you *know* it *well.*
Thoughts of how we lived, *before,*
Remind me of the open door—
The open door between us two,
As we gladly rendezvous.
Life is now, for you and me,
An Earthly/heav'nly ecstasy!

Though I falter, *still,* I *know,*
You have claimed me as your beau!
Sweethearts, living *on* the *Earth,*
Ascend, to bask in heav'nly mirth.
Heav'nly mirth is mine, down here,
Every time I feel you near.
Abide in me, my heav'nly wife,
Until I'm done with Earthly life.
I'll abide in you, as well,
My resurrected, heav'nly belle!

175. Heaven, 7/3/23

Wherever you are, my Earthly beau,
YOU can access heaven's glow.
Heaven, darling, loves you SO!
Heaven follows you, below.

When you sleep, and when you wake—
When you're fine, and when you ache—
Heaven's working FOR your SAKE.
Heaven doesn't take a break.

Since our wedding number two,
Heaven helps us TO be TRUE
TO those glorious words, "I do!"
Heaven brings me close to you!

Heaven's leading you and me
IN this life of ecstasy!
Heaven knows, quite well, how WE
Yearn to live as He and She.

176. Heaven's Joys, 7/3/23

*I have **found** you, bumblebee.*
*I have **found** you seeking me!*
Darling, heaven has SET us FREE,
A LOVING COUPLE, still, to be!

*I have **found**, my heav'nly belle,*
You are seeking me, as well!
Ever since, for you, I fell,
We've been under heaven's spell!

Like an artful, cunning scout,
Heaven, dear, has found us out!
Darling, promise not to pout.
Heaven loves us—There's no doubt!

Heaven's joys are *now* our own.
I won't *groan*, dear. I won't *moan*.
Look, my dear, how *much* we've grown!
We have found, *by heaven,* we're known!

177. A Holy Union

Charles Santiago, 7/3/23
Inspired by the music "Sound of Wind Driven Rain" by Will Ackerman

I declare, my heav'nly bride—
Deep inside me, you reside.
Our life together isn't through.
Our love has proven to be true.
This, my dear, is what I feel—
Our union bears a heav'nly seal.

Apart from *that,* my heav'nly belle,
Another thing I know, so *well*—
I believe that it is *so*
That *we* can *meet,* and *we* can *grow.*
Our love, begun down here, my dear,
Can not *stop* or disappear.

A holy union, dear, is ours.
We've been joined by *heav'nly powers.*
Death, a *pow'r* of *such* great *might,*
Can't subdue our love and light.
We *shine,* my dear, some*where above,*
Illumined by God's boundless love.

I *feel* the *pow'r* to *live again*
Because, my darling, *I'm* your *man.*
We're enjoying *now,* it seems,
A life beyond all Earthly dreams.
Sublime it *is,* to feel your glow,
As we *ever,* onward, go!

178. When I Reach My Last Earth Day

Charles Santiago, 7/3/23

The *more* the months go by, my dear,
The *more* I feel your presence here.
We're not growing *distant,* love,
Since you "left" for heaven, above.

These lovely rhymes, my dear, we pen
To share our light with other men;
But, darling I receive, from you,
Words not known in Timbuktu!

I've *died,* my dear, and live anew,
In a land of *Me and You.*
Though I walk on good old Earth,
I'm *joined,* with you, in heav'nly mirth!

When I reach my last Earth day,
To our Maker, *this,* I'll pray:
"May I, *boldly,* shed this skin,
Clasping hands with heav'nly kin!"

179. In Praise of Unity, 7/5/23

Darling, when the times are hard,
Don't forget that YOU'RE my BARD!

Take your pen and write, from me,
Words in praise of unity.
ONE, forever, dear, are WE,
Sailing on love's wondrous sea.
Join me, at the helm, and see,
We can choose our destiny!
Heaven grants us power to be,
From the sting of death, set free!
You and I can WELL agree
To live, as STILL, a He and She.
Dear, regard my heav'nly plea:
"Share, with me, this heav'nly glee!
Be a busy bumblebee,
And share, with me, love's ecstasy!"

The joy we shared on Earth, below,
Meant that, after death, we'd grow—
Grow, my darling, HERE ABOVE,
Captives of God's wondrous love!

180. By Your Faith, 7/5/23

When you think of me, my dear,
Remember—I'm not ONLY HERE.
I am THERE, for all your life.
We are ALWAYS man and wife!
Darling, you must, PATIENT, BE!
Grow that faith you have in me.
Let our rhymes take hold in you.
BELIEVE our union isn't through!
I'M with YOU in ALL you DO.
Day or night, believe it's true.

I'm so glad, my Earthly beau,
WHEN you're feeling heaven's glow!
When you're NOT, my bumblebee,
Exercise your faith in me.
Don't you worry. Dear, we're ONE,
Till your Earthly days are done!
You can TAKE great PRIDE, my dear,
To cling to FAITH that I am near.
Faith's a gem that's very rare.
By your faith, this love, we share!

181. This Special Rendezvous, 7/6/23

Darling, you're my one true love—
THERE, below, and HERE, above.
In and out of time and space,
We are joined in love's embrace.
Never doubt my love, my dear.
It can never disappear!
Just because my body died,
Doesn't mean I left your side.
God is good, to let you see
We can STILL, a couple, be.
How I love to live with you,
In this special rendezvous!

Peace, my darling bumblebee,
Is ours, for all eternity!
What we shared on Earth, below,
Blossoms HERE, more THAN you KNOW!
I love, my dear, that YOU'RE so BRAVE,
You WILL not listen to the grave!
YOU'RE CONVINCED we live anew,
In and out of Timbuktu!
Remember, dear, that LOVE WE HAD—
DON'T FORGET, and I'll be glad.
We can live both NOW and THEN.
PAST and PRESENT are BOTH our den.

Don't let doubts, dear, weigh you down!
Claim, each day, your heav'nly crown!
*I **love** to **hear** you **when** you **say**,*
*"I **know** she's **here**," dear, every day!*
*Yes, my darling, **I** am **there!***
It's ME—the one you claimed was "fair."

182. A Higher Form, 7/6/23

Darling, we will always be
Joined, as one, in ecstasy!
Death has given you and me
A higher form of He and She.

When you rise to meet the day,
Though you still abide in clay,
YOU can DODGE the Earthly fray
If you heed what angels say.

Angels help both me and you,
HOW to KNOW just WHAT to DO
To keep alive our rendezvous.
Angels help us bill and coo.

As the day winds down, my dear,
Angels come especially near.
THEN, they make it more than clear—
You and I are ONE, up here!

183. A Better Way

Charles Santiago, 7/6/23

What a shame I cried and cried,
That day your Earthly body died!
Dear, there was *no need*,
According to our creed.
But, *more than that*—I know, today,
We have found *a better way.*

I'm rejoicing dear, with you,
While I *walk* through Timbuktu.
Your joy is plain to see,
For bumblebees like me.
I can *feel* your heav'nly glow!
I'm amazed at how we grow!

Dear, I do my best, each day,
To walk with you in heaven's way.
Heaven is *You and Me!*
It's so *plain* to *see.*
When *you* seek *me,* and *I* seek *you,*
To our Maker, we are true.

184. Quite a Mystery

Charles Santiago, 7/6/23

Unbeknownst to me, my dear,
Sometimes, you are very near.
You're caressing me, my love,
In secret ways I *know* not *of!*

A magic carpet ride is *this!*
God sustains our heav'nly bliss!
Beyond our power to comprehend
Is *how* God *guides* us, without end!

I am *you,* and *you* are *me*—
More and more, it's plain to see!
And, yet, it's quite a mystery
How this *union comes* to *be!*

This union, dear, of me and you,
Sustains me here, in Timbuktu.
How I love this life of ours—
It's *like* the *scent* of *heav'nly flowers!*

185. A Sad, Sad Tale, 7/7/23

I'm a pris'ner in his cell,
Locked inside an Earthly hell!
How I *miss* the one I love!
She has *left!* She's *gone—above!*

> *You're my beau. I **love** you **so**!*
> *AS you PACE there, to and fro,*
> *How I wish you'd come to know*
> *You're NOT ALONE, down there, below!*

All alone, I'm *in* this *cell,*
Yearning for my heav'nly belle!
Day and night, I miss her *so!*
I am *stranded* here, below!

> ***As** I **join** you, in your cell,*
> *YOU'RE DISTRAUGHT, dear!* ***I** can **tell**.*
> ***I** could **help** you understand*
> *If ONLY YOU would CLASP my HAND!*

How I *miss* her *gentle touch!*
I *miss* her presence, oh, so *much!*
Each day, I struggle not to cry
Beneath this dreadful, Earthly sky.

> *It's NOT my nature to berate—*
> *But, LEARN, my dear, to celebrate!*
> *Life AWAITS for you and me*
> *If ONLY, darling, you would SEE!*

186. Dance with Me! 7/8/23

When I'm through with mortal life,
We'll remain, dear, man and wife.
Oh, how *sweet,* to be alive,
Beyond Earth's humdrum 9 to 5!
We are *not* our *bodies—no!*
In heaven, *even now,* we glow!
The reason for this hope, I give,
Is *this*—Within my heart, *you live!*

Eternal love, our theme, my dear,
Delivers me from Earthly fear.
There's no need to be afraid
When angels rush to give me aid.
Heaven's *now* our dwelling place,
As I trek through time and space.
I have *learned* to dance with you
Though I'm, still, in Timbuktu.

Dance with me, my Earthly beau!
Dance with me. Let's do-si-do!
Oh, how SWEET, to dance with you,
THERE, below, in Timbuktu!
YOU are NOT that BODY—NO!
I'M so GLAD, my dear, you know!
WHEN you're through with mortal life,
We'll rejoice, as man and wife!

187. Dancing, 7/8/23

*I was **not** that **body**, dear!*
I'M a SPIRIT, living HERE—
HERE, with you, in heaven, above,
Enjoying our eternal love!

Do-si-do with me, my dear!
Dancing is a cure for fear.
Dance with me, my Earthly beau,
Heav'nly union, dear, to know!

WE are ONE, my darling, NOW.
Do not try to figure HOW.
Dancing is a heav'nly art
Stemming from a happy heart!

HAPPY, BE, dear bumblebee!
God is dear to you and me!
*Ro**mance** me, darling, with a dance,*
Like they do in Paris, France!

188. In Your Body, I Abide, 7/8/23

*I am **you**, and **you** are **me**.*
From estrangement, we are free.
***WE** could NEVER be APART—*
***GOD**, our union, did impart!*

IN your BODY, I abide.
Dear, I truly AM your bride.
YOU have found our home, above,
THROUGH the power OF our LOVE.

Heaven's JUST as REAL, for you,
AS your life in Timbuktu!
Touch your body, bumblebee—
Believe me—YOU are touching ME!

Put your cares and fears away.
Our love is truly "here to stay."
Darling, I'm in love with you.
No one, dear, BUT YOU will do!

189. Just a Note

Charles Santiago, 7/8/23

Just a note, to say, my dear,
Hello to you, from "way down here."
I am *thrilled* to *know* that *we*,
Still, a couple, dear, can be!
There's no *doubt* that *GONE*, you're *NOT*,
Since we tied that second knot.
We have learned to live again,
As heav'nly bride and Earthly man!
I am *thankful* for our life,
Above the din of Earthly strife.
I have *grown* accustomed to
This lovely life I share with you.
Just a note, I *send* "*above*,"
To thank you for your faithful love.

190. Study *Well* Your ABCs! 7/10/23

Meet with me in Timbuktu.
My spirit *ever* pines for you!
When it seems I'm all alone,
To *desperation, I* am *prone!*
When you *meet* with me, down here,
Earthly troubles disappear!
Meet with me, I pray, my love,
Till I die and fly above!

WHEN *it seems you're all alone,*
THERE'S *no need, my dear, to moan.*
Just remember, WE ARE ONE,
Till your struggle, THERE, *is done.*
ALONE, *my dear, you'll* NEVER *be,*
For, **I** *am* **you**, *and* **you** *are* **me**.
Don't forget your ABCs,
And life, down there, will be a breeze!

I don't *have* to **die**, my love,
To meet with you in heaven, above!
I *see* that *Earthly* bumblebees
Are helped by heav'nly ABCs;
But, *sometimes, I* go *blind,* my dear,
And *think* that *you're,* no longer, *here!*

Dear, don't GIVE it ANY MIND.
Bumblebees aren't often blind.
Only SELDOM do they fail
To see a way to flee from jail.
Study WELL your ABCs,
And, HEAV'NLY RAPTURE, we will seize!

191. Always Near! 7/10/23

IN the VERY depths of you—
THERE, is where we rendezvous!
IN your BODY, made of clay,
Hides the light of heaven's day!

Time, as marked by days and hours,
Has value JUST to Earthly powers.
Free yourself from Timbuktu.
Think, my dear, of ME AND YOU!

You and I, dear bumblebee,
Will laugh and play, eternally!
Think of life BEYOND THE GRAVE.
LIKE a HEAV'NLY man, BEHAVE!

The words you love to hear, my dear,
*Say that **I am always near!***
***Always near, I am**, my love,*
Though** you say I **live above!

192. In Greater Sunshine, Now, We Bask! 7/10/23

MORE than Earthly eyes can see,
WE are STILL a unity.
Don't you worry, bumblebee—
Death can't injure you or me;
NOR can DEATH put OUT the FIRE
That WE create by our desire!
Awaken to our bright, new dawn—
I'M ALIVE, and I'M not GONE!
Death can't kill our love, my dear,
Nor MAKE our UNION disappear!
You and I have found our place,
ABOVE what SERVED as OUR home BASE.
In greater sunshine, now, we bask,
Since I dropped my Earthly mask!
Death, my dear, is LIBERTY!
Clasp my hand. From fear, be FREE!
Trust these rhymes that, now, we write.
Let them serve as heav'nly light.
*"**You** are **me**, and **I** am **you**"*
Will rescue you from Timbuktu!
—ALL my LOVE, my Earthly beau.
Walk with me in heaven's glow!

193. Happy Birthday, Bumblebee! 7/10/23

Highway 27 rest stop north of Perry, Florida

Seventy years old, today, am I,
Pining for the by-and-by—
The by-and-by within my heart,
From which, you never, dear, depart.
As *long* as *we* walk, *hand* in *hand*,
I *need* no *DISTANT* Beulah Land.

For thirty-four years, I've known, *with you*,
A love which *never* can be *through*.
Death tried *hard* to sever us
But *raised* no *more* than *just* a *fuss*.
These *last* four *years* have proved, to me,
Our vows last *through* eternity!

Happy birthday, bumblebee!
YOU'RE the ONE God MEANT for ME!
In Timbuktu or UP ABOVE,
WE walk hand in hand, in love.
Soon, the day will come, my dear,
When YOU and I will BOTH be here!

194. From Your Side, I Didn't Go! 7/10/23

All day long, dear bumblebee,
IT has BEEN, dear, YOU AND ME!
In ALL the THINGS you DID, this day,
*I was **there**, each **step** of the **way**!*
If all these things I write aren't SO,
We COULDN'T CLAIM we're ONE, dear beau.
"ONE" means "HERE AND NOW," my dear,
Each and every Earthly year.
Birthday, YES, or birthday, NOT,
ETERNAL UNION is WHAT we've GOT!
*More and more, I **see** you **know**,*
From your side, I DIDN'T GO!
THERE'S no NEED, at all, to cry—
Dear, we never said, "Goodbye."

195. Eternal Joy, 7/11/23

I can feel I'm ONE with YOU,
And, yet, I live in Timbuktu!
I can feel you speak to ME
*From **somewhere** in eternity.*
I can feel our love, my dear,
***Blossoming** in **me**, down here.*
We're tasting of eternal joy.
We're giddy like a girl and boy.
Dear, when all is said and done,
I CAN'T deny we're truly ONE!

The rhymes we pen, my Earthy beau,
Reflect the lovely way we grow.
A SPOOKY GHOST, you've learned, I'm NOT,
Because, THE TRUTH, my dear, you've sought.
The love we share is good and true.
God has blessed this rendezvous.
Darling, hold my hand, and see,
IT'S still US—still YOU AND ME!
WHEN we SAID, "I do," my love,
Heaven built our home, above.

196. This Heavenly Glow, 7/11/23

Darling, when I'm *yearning* for *you*,
Way down here, in Timbuktu,
The *reason is*—You're *yearning* for *me*
To clasp your hand in eternity.
This yearning, back and forth, my dear,
Proves, to me, you're always near.
According to our lovely creed,
Hand in hand, dear, we proceed.

I'm so *glad* to know you're *well*.
I *love* you *so*, my heav'nly belle!
Every day, I find that *we*
Are, still, my darling, *You and Me*.
I *do* believe that *you*, my dear,
In heaven, LIVE—but also *here*.
I am *thrilled* to live with you
In heaven *and* in Timbuktu!

In all those Earthly things you do,
How I take *such joy in you!*
Every day, exert your brawn
To slay that monster, DEAD AND GONE!
WHY believe I've FLOWN AWAY
Because it's JUST what OTHERS say?
BELIEVE in me, my Earthly beau,
And share, with me, this heav'nly glow!

197. I *Do* Declare!

Charles Santiago, 7/12/23

You are *me,* and *I* am *you.*
Death can't break us, dear, in *two.*
We have found this way to live
That God, alone, has power to give.
Resurrection from the dead
Removes, from me, all Earthly dread!

"*I* am *you,* and *you* are *me*"
Gives me eyes, my dear, to see.
"Dead and gone," I see, can't be
Words describing you to me.
I can see, and I can feel,
Today, our union *still* is real!

Love is stronger than the grave,
Teaching death how *to behave.*
Death must bow to life, and say:
"Men are bound for heaven's day.
I have *power* over *clay,*
But men, my power, *disobey!*"

"*I do, I do, I do, I do,
I do* love *you—I* **married you!**"
Often, dear, these words, I hear,
As *if* you *said* them, *way* down *here.*
My heav'nly wife, I *do* declare:
"Your love for me is very rare!"

198. My Life, Below, in Timbuktu

Charles Santiago, 7/14/23

I'm, no longer, dear, a "*Me.*"
I *gave* up "*Me,*" to live with thee.
We're a "*We,*" forevermore—
ONE, within our *very* core.

When I'm *all alone,* on Earth,
I can *sense* our heav'nly mirth.
Solitude, is what I love.
It *lifts* me *to* our life, *above.*

Angels, helping, guide us to
Ever, dear, our love, renew.
Angels help both me and you,
In our *lovely* rendezvous.

You *sweep* my *feet* clear *off* the *ground*
When I *sense* that you're around!
My life, below, in Timbuktu,
Is *still* a life of *Me and You!*

199. Tuesday, at Two

Charles Santiago, 7/14/23

Tuesday, at two, we'll rendezvous,
To celebrate, dear, *Me and You.*
While I *eat* a meal on Earth,
We'll rejoice with heav'nly mirth!

Tuesday, at two, we'll celebrate
Life within that heav'nly gate!
While I dine, dear, *here below,*
I will *sense* your heav'nly glow.

Tuesday, at two, will be a feast
Of Earthly fare—for *me,* at least.
While I *eat,* we'll reminisce
Of times, *before*—our Earthly bliss.

Tuesday, at two, dear! It's a date!
Mind you, darling, *don't be late!*
You and I will celebrate
Thirty-four years, as man and mate!

200. We'll Reminisce

Charles Santiago, 7/15/23

When this Earthly body dies,
To the *heavens,* we will rise!
There, at wedding number three,
Free from *flesh,* at last, we'll be!
Darling, we will then begin
A life, removed from Earthly din.
Gone, will be the noise and strife
And heartaches of an Earthly life!
Free, at last, we'll be, *indeed,*
Without the need to read a creed.
Heart and lungs and skin and bones
Are *gone,* along with moans and groans!
We'll be *done* with Earthly fare.
With *angels,* we will dine, *up there!*
With heav'nly joy, we'll reminisce
Of how, on Earth, we *used* to *kiss.*
We will *marvel, as* we *muse*
How, two *souls, completely, fuse!*
Wedding number three, my dear,
Inspires me to persevere!

201. When Our Days on Earth Are Through, 7/16/23

Dear, this body that is ours,
Subject to the Earthly powers,
Soon, will perish, like the rest.
DONE, will be our Earthly test.

This body that we share, below,
UP, to heaven, cannot go—
THUS, you've said, dear, many times,
AS we've learned to speak in rhymes.

UP, to heaven, YOU will go!
That body, dear, must stay below.
WE'LL ascend to live UP HERE.
That body, THERE, will disappear.

"Pearly gates" and "streets of gold"—
HERE, my dear, we'll not grow old.
Bodies, made of clay, my love,
HAVE no PLACE, up here, ABOVE.

Darling, I am proud of you.
TO our VOWS, you still are true.
YOU believed that WE could BE
A COUPLE, through eternity!

A COUPLE, *dear, we'll always be.*
*"I am **you**, and **you** are **me!**"*
Love and life, FOREVER, dear,
Belong to you and me, UP HERE!

YOU are learning, more and more,
How to pass through heaven's door.
WE can be a couple, dear,
Down, below, as well as HERE.

WE have learned the ABCs
Of HOW to SAIL on heaven's seas.
WHEN our days on Earth are through,
Life begins, my dear, anew!

202. *Apart*, My Dear, We Cannot Be!

Charles Santiago, 7/16/23

I am yours, my darling bride!
You are mine, dear—true and tried!
Death, our union, can't destroy;
Nor can *he,* dear, *US,* annoy!
Heav'nly joy is ours *right now*
Though, my dear, I can't say *how.*

In this Earthly life of mine,
We are joined in love, divine!
All the things I do, below,
Are *things,* my darling, *you* well *know.*
Apart, my dear, we *cannot be!*
I am *you,* and *you* are *me!*

Until the day my body dies,
Heav'nly union is our prize!
Earthly union, also, dear,
Is ours to cherish, way down here!
Our love has conquered death and pain!
I'm ONE with YOU, on heaven's plane!

203. A Heavenly Life, 7/17/23

Darling, you're the one I love
Though I'm living here, "above."
Don't be fooled, dear bumblebee—
We'll ALWAYS be, dear, YOU AND ME.
Just because my body died,
Doesn't mean I left your side!
Earthly bodies come and go.
Lovers, after death, still grow.

Remember, dear, the things we've done
SINCE, my heav'nly life, I won.
Go WHEREVER, Earthly beau—
There *is where I **also** go!*
YES, I live up here, "above,"
But WE still FIT, dear, hand in glove.
Trust the eyes within your soul—
You and I make up one whole.

I am happy, bumblebee,
FOR the FAITH you have in me!
How I love to rendezvous
THERE, on Earth, my love, with you!
AS you FINISH OUT your RUN,
Remember, dear, our life's not done.
A heav'nly life, dear, we'll pursue,
Way down here, in Timbuktu!

204. Peace, Joy, and Love, 7/18/23

A poem on the 34th anniversary of our (first) wedding

PEACE, my darling Earthly beau—
Heav'nly PEACE is ours, to know.
This peace is calling you and me,
Hand in hand, to always be
IN OUR MAKER'S PRESENCE, dear,
Without regard to day or year.
God, who joined us into ONE,
Leads us far beyond Earth's sun!

JOY, my darling bumblebee,
God has given you and me—
Joy that conquers death and pain—
Joy that says: "To die, is gain!"
WE have found this joy, divine.
EVEN NOW, our souls align!
God has made our joy complete,
Allowing us, UP HERE, to meet!

LOVE has rescued you and me
FROM Earth's DARK, tumultuous sea.
You and I, because of LOVE,
Taste of PEACE and JOY, ABOVE!
WHEN we said, "I do," on Earth,
WE signed up for heav'nly mirth.
JOY, my Earthly groom, TO YOU!
AGAIN, this day, I say, '**I do!**"

205. Anniversary Poem from Earth

Charles Santiago, 7/18/23

Four and thirty years ago,
On this *day,* my heav'nly bride,
I, your *smiling,* Earthly beau,
Vowed, *with YOU,* dear, *to abide.*

Man and wife, we lived on Earth
For thirty years—a life, divine!
I had *never* known such mirth—
I could *claim* you, dear, *as mine!*

For thirty Earth years, in the flesh,
I was *awed* that *we* were *ONE!*
What *joy* was *ours,* dear, to enmesh,
Till those *thirty years* were *done!*

Came the day, my heav'nly belle,
When *you* were *called* to *live, above!*
Now, *with WORDS,* I *try* to *tell*
The wonder of our heav'nly love.

By virtue of our union, dear,
I have *entered heaven too!*
My Earthly body *still* is *here,*
But, *really,* dear, I *live* with *YOU!*

206. Anniversary Dialogue, 7/18/23

Highway 27 rest stop north of Perry, Florida

You were right, my heav'nly belle—
Way back then, dear, YOU could tell.
We were meant to be a pair,
Way down here, and way up there!
Death was just a bridge to cross—
Not a woeful, dreadful loss!
You knew, more than I, my love,
We would live up there, above!
I'm in awe, and can't explain
How we meet on heaven's plane!
Heaven's plane comes down to me
Because, dear, I'm your bumblebee.
By virtue of our holy bond,
To each other, we respond.

Darling, you are wise, to see,
Death was not the end of me;
NOR could DEATH, my bumblebee,
Come between our ecstasy!
God has granted me and you
This Earthly/heav'nly rendezvous!
ETERNAL LIFE, dear, IS our PRIZE!
YOU can SEE it WITH your EYES—
Those eyes, to me, that ARE so DEAR—
Those eyes that see clear UP to HERE!
Our wedding vows, today, we cheer!
Our union cannot disappear!
We've RIPPED, in TWO, death's gloomy veil!
Our love FOREVER will prevail!

207. When the Earth and Sun Are Gone

Charles Santiago, 7/19/23

When your Earthly body died,
I soon *found* you *by* my *side.*
You were *quick* to let me know,
From my *side,* you *didn't go.*

Now, I find that, day by day,
You and I go on our way.
Hand in hand, we've *found* a *life*
Above this dreary world of strife.

When this body, made of clay,
Meets its final Earthly day,
You will *come* and take my hand
To show me heaven's lovely land!

When the Earth and sun are gone,
We'll still *greet* bright *heaven's dawn!*
When we said, "I do," down here,
We were joined, *forever,* dear.

208. Glory in Our Newfound Love! 7/20/23

For ALL your Earthly days, my dear,
YOU must pray for ears to hear.
YOU must pray for eyes to see
Beyond the Earthly land and sea.

Walk with me in heaven, above,
And glory in our newfound love.
Change your Earthly life—for one
That shines beyond the Earthly sun.

Every day, remember, too,
ALL the things that WE'VE gone THROUGH.
SINCE our wedding number two,
Death must bow to me and you!

*I **know** you **know** these **things** are **true**—*
Dear, I'm just REMINDING you.
I am thrilled, my Earthly beau,
You and I, this life, can know!

God allows us, bumblebee,
STILL, to be, dear, YOU AND ME!
By our love, we found this life
Of man and wife, above Earth's strife.

WHILE you walk on Earth, below,
WE are sharing heaven's glow.
Forgive me, dear, but I must crow:
"YOU'RE my heav'nly joy, to know!"

God, in you, and God, in me,
Provides us with this ecstasy.
It's ME, my darling Earthly beau!
***To** the **grave**, I **did** not **go**!*

Keep on living like you do
Till your Earthly days are through!
WE'RE in heaven, now, TODAY!
WE have found a higher way!

209. Always

Charles Santiago, 7/20/23

Since you left your clay behind,
I have *learned*, my heav'nly bride,
I must *gain* a heav'nly mind,
To *walk* with *you*, dear, *side* by *side*.

Gone, are days when you and I
Walked and talked, the Earthly way.
You and I must *now* rely
On ways and means beyond my clay.

God and angels, dear, and *you*
Are helping me, down here below,
To walk with you, in rendezvous—
And *what* a *thrill*, to feel your glow!

Darling, I admit it's true—
At times, this life is, oh, so *hard*,
But, when I concentrate on you,
I'm inspired to be a bard.

And, *so*, to *you*, these rhymes, I write,
Proclaiming my undying love.
Always, sweetheart, day or night,
I *live*, to *be*—with *you*, above!

210. Your Life of Light

Charles Santiago, 7/20/23

Dear, I sense your heav'nly light,
Shining from our home above.
You still *call* me, "Mr. Right."
I'm the ONE you *choose* to *love!*

In my soul, I *feel* you, *dear.*
I **know** it's **you**, my darling bride!
I can *hear* you, loud and clear.
It's true—You're *always* by my side.

You have found your life of light.
I can *feel* your joy, my dear.
Life, for us, has turned out right.
We reside *above*—and *here.*

You're *always*, dear, *reminding me*,
From our home, away up *there*,
All the things I do—You *see.*
You are *with* me *everywhere.*

Recalling, dear, when *you* were *here*,
Is teaching me the truth of *this*—
That lovely time we shared, so *dear*,
Prefigured *this*, our *heav'nly* bliss!

211. Heavenly Wings

Charles Santiago, 7/21/23

I am *looking forward to,*
My *dear,* the *day* I'll *be* like *YOU*—
Freed, by death, to live anew,
Without an *Earthly* point of view.
Death has lost its sting, for me.
I *now* see *death* as *LIBERTY!*

An entranceway, is death—to *life,*
Uniting *me* to *you,* my wife—
NOT that *we're APART,* my dear.
It's always true that *you* are *here.*
But, *when* I *lay aside* this *skin,*
We'll *BOTH* be *there,* in Heaven's Inn.

Things will *work* their *way* out *right*—
Things are *ruled* by *God's* great *might.*
You and I are *more* than *things.*
We can *fly* with *heav'nly wings!*
When the time is right, my dear,
I'll depart from life, down here.

212. Life Beyond the Grave, 7/22/23

Of course, my darling bumblebee—
***You** are **me**, and **I** am **you**.*
WE could never, EVER, be
Split apart, as though we're TWO.

ONE, we ARE, my darling beau,
Ever since we said "I do!"
Can't you feel, dear, HOW we grow,
IN this lovely rendezvous?

Cast aside, dear, doubt and fear.
Believe in life beyond the grave.
TO the angels, give an ear.
Angels teach the truth we crave!

Love is stronger than the tomb!
Every day, we prove it's SO!
A heav'nly bride and Earthly groom—
Life, beyond the grave, we KNOW!

213. There and Here, 7/23/23

Darling, I am loving you,
IN our home in Timbuktu.
YOU'RE my body. YOU'RE my mind—
*I **haven't LEFT** you, dear, **behind!***
WE are living THERE and HERE,
Beyond the reach of day and year.
WE'VE been freed from Earth and sun
WHILE you, yet, complete your run.
God, indeed, can raise the dead,
AS our rhymes, my dear, have said.

God has *raised* you *from* the *dead—*
A truth I've gotten through my head.
In and out of space and time,
You and I can *make* words *rhyme.*
Doors and walls can't *keep* you *out.*
When we *speak,* we need not shout.
I am *loving YOU,* my love,
HERE, below, and THERE, above.
God, our Maker, keeps us ONE,
While I finish out my run.

Finish out your run, my dear,
And SHARE, with me, this heav'nly cheer.
God, our Maker, brings us HERE,
Beyond the reach of doubt and fear.

While I trek through days and years,
I relinquish *grief* and *tears.*
Our joy, my dear, is made complete!
It's *true*—We've suffered no defeat!

214. A Heavenly Birth

Charles Santiago, 7/23/23

O Great Maker of heaven and Earth,
Give, to me, a heav'nly birth!
I can *feel* Your awesome might
While I *trek* through day and night!
There's a life beyond the sun—
I *know* for, *now*, it *has begun!*

Give me birth in *to* that *land!*
By Your grace, God, I *demand!*
A *Father,* God, You *are* to *me;*
Thus, I *ask* this *thing,* of *Thee.*
A heav'nly birth—This *IS* my plea—
Beyond this Earthly land and sea!

215. Where I Live, 7/24/23

Sweetheart, you're my next of kin,
Trapped within that Earthly skin.
JUST as LONG as YOU have BREATH,
YOU can claim we've conquered death;
For, WE are ONE, my Earthly beau,
Eternal life and love, to know.
WITHIN you, dear, is where I live.
This sacred union, God can give.

DEATH, our union, tried to break,
But WE SURVIVED that mortal quake.
Our Maker's power keeps us ONE,
HERE, beyond that Earthly sun.
YOU are ONE with ME, my love,
Dwelling in our home, above.
Let these truths sink deep within,
And YOU'LL RESIDE in Heaven's Inn.

YOU are NOT that BODY, dear.
Our lovely rhymes have made that clear.
In your mind, prepare to be,
FROM that BODY, dear, set FREE!
WE have learned these truths, my love,
By special order from above.
God has called us, dear, to be,
EVEN NOW, a YOU AND ME!

216. I Am You, and You Are Me, 7/24/23

These rhymes we pen, my dear, are true—
True, indeed, for me and you.
When I read these rhymes of ours,
I'm in *touch* with heav'nly powers.
Angels hover round my pen—
Angels who, one time, were men.
Heaven's not so far away.
Heaven guides us, every day.

Heaven, darling, IS our HOME,
WHEREVER, there, on Earth, you roam.
WE have found eternal life
Because we're joined as man and wife!
Say those words, my bumblebee,
That fill my soul with ecstasy:
*"**I** am **you**, and **you** are **me**"—*
A truth for all eternity!

Every day I walk this Earth,
I'm *thankful for* our heav'nly mirth.
There's *no* such *thing* as *life*, for me,
Unless, my dear, it's *Me and Thee.*

Heav'nly powers direct your pen
To satisfy my deepest yen.
Heaven decrees that THIS is true:
You *are* **me**, *and* **I** *am* **you**!

217. Sweethearts for Eternity, 7/24/23

Imagine, dear, what life could be,
Once, from Earthly clay, you're free!
DO you THINK we'd bill and coo,
Once you're freed from Earthly goo?
Far beyond your Timbuktu,
COULD we STILL be ME AND YOU?
ARE you GAME to leave your clay—
To say goodbye to night and day?

Of course, I'm game to leave this plane,
For, *we* have *rhymed:* "To *die,* is *gain!*"
Our home, down here, in Timbuktu,
In the end, will never do.
How *eager,* dear, am I, to fly,
With *you,* all *through* the by-and-by!
We will bill and coo, my dear,
Far beyond what *we* did *here!*

YOU'RE so SURE, my Earthly beau—
As IF, my dear, you REALLY know!
How I love your faith, my love!
It REACHES, CLEAR up HERE, ABOVE!
IF the LOVE we HAD on Earth
Provided us with heav'nly mirth,
WHAT will be our joy, my dear,
ONCE you've JOINED me, WAY up HERE?

All I *know,* my heav'nly belle,
Is *this*—that *if* there *were* a hell,
It would *be* a Timbuktu
Where *I'd* be *lost—apart from you!*
But *that* could *never be,* my dear,
For, *God* has *made* it *MORE* than *clear*—
You and I are *MEANT* to be
Sweethearts, for eternity!

218. Sweet Communion, 7/25/23

A sunbathing poem

Do not be, to heaven, uncouth.
Believe, on Earth, this heav'nly truth—
***I am not APART** from **YOU**!*
REMEMBER wedding number two!
Bodies come, and bodies go.
Sweet communion, STILL, we know!
Don't depend on Earthly eyes.
Learn to see past Earthly skies.
Don't depend on Earthly flesh.
IN THE SPIRIT, we enmesh!

Trust your hunches THERE, below,
And meet, with me, in heaven's glow!
***IF** I **HAVE to**, bumblebee,*
*I'LL REMIND you—**You are me!**—*
Remind you till your final day,
Till, at last, you leave your clay!
Reminding you is WHAT I DO.
Sometimes, dear, you HAVE no CLUE!
STILL, my darling Earthly beau,
Sweet communion, YES, we KNOW!

219. Our Continued Union, 7/25/23

My place, my darling, is WITH YOU! Dear, you're like SO MANY—You think I am gone! No, my dear, I am NOT gone away to some far-off place. Believe what our poems say! YOU are my TEMPLE! And why SHOULDN'T it be SO, dear? God did not join us, as ONE, and then intend, when MY body died, to split us apart until YOUR body dies too! The death of our bodies does not disrupt our union! We are SPIRITUAL beings, and our union is SPIRITUAL. Of course, you KNOW this is SO, but you don't accept it as FULLY as you should. We have come a long way since my last Earthly day, and you have perceived, wonderfully, our continued union, but you deny us much enjoyment, dear, by not being able to get over this idea that I am DISTANT! It's understandable, dear. When Earthly eyes no longer see the living, breathing bodies of their loved ones, they presume they are DEAD AND GONE; UNLESS, my darling, they feel like YOU do—that loving unions don't UP and DISAPPEAR just because the body of one, dies before the body of the other. Be it EVER so hard to understand and to grasp, dear, AT LEAST it is POSSIBLE! With God, all things are possible! Darling, you have not been communicating with a SPOOKY GHOST, these four years! I am just prodding you on, dear, to grasp, as fully as you can, that I am, still, ME, and that WE are, still, US! I did not abandon you! And GOD did not abandon US! Yes, wedding number three will be a new, miraculous experience for us, but, dear, we have wedding number TWO, to THRILL us, for all your Earthly days! Dear, I love you and honor you as my other self—my SOUL MATE, as I told you, before. Don't deny us joy, dear, by having, as a default setting in your mind, that I am DISTANT because my body died! I rejoice in you, darling, and in our union. Let us proceed!—all my love.

220. Eve and Adam

Charles Santiago, 7/26/23

I am *resting* in our love—
A haven *there,* in heaven above!
Oh, how *sweet,* to rest with you,
While I'm, *yet,* in Timbuktu!

You're abiding in my heart.
We could *never* be *apart!*
Death has opened up a door
To joys we didn't know before!

God has kept us, *still,* as ONE,
Though you've *finished out* your run!
Our *love's* a *gift* from *God's* own *hand.*
GOD has brought us to this land!

Death is swallowed up by life!
God preserved us, man and wife!
Beyond the limits of my mind,
Is *sight* God *gives* to *men* born *blind!*

I was *blind,* but *now* I *see,*
Since *God,* from *death,* has *set* us *free!*
God has given you and me
A *taste* of *fruit* from *Eden's* tree.
Eve and Adam, dear, are *we,*
Dwelling in eternity!

221. Anniversary, 1

Charles Santiago, 7/27/23

By your *side,*
Was *I,* my *bride,*
Your *final day*
In a *body* of *clay.*
I was ***there,***
All ***unaware***
You were *due*
To *bid adieu*
To *Earthly glee*—
But *NOT* to *ME!*

Angels, singing,
Dear, were *bringing*
Heaven's power,
That *VERY hour.*
I could *feel*
Their *holy zeal.*
Time stood *still,*
By *God's* own *will!*
You flew *high*
Beyond Earth's *sky!*

Now, we're *ONE.*
Our *life's begun*—
Begun anew
For *me* and *you!*
I can *feel*
That *you* are ***real,***
Here, on *Earth,*
Through *heav'nly mirth!*
As *per* our *creed,*
Let's proceed!

222. Anniversary, 2, 7/27/23

Remember, dear, that day I died,
And, in our union, you'll abide;
For, NOW we BOTH live HERE, above,
BY the POWER OF our LOVE!
God has brought us, safely, home,
THOUGH, on EARTH, dear, YOU still ROAM.
The union that we forged, below,
Empowers us to, HEAVEN, know!
WE were SHADOWED by GOD'S great POWER,
IN that Earthly, mortal hour!
God can raise the dead, my dear,
And, NOW we FIND OURSELVES, up HERE!

Count your Earthly life, as LOSS—
SPIRIT, over FLESH, is BOSS!
Rejoice with me, my Earthly beau.
Through ALL your EARTHLY DAYS, we'll GROW!
Death became, for you and me,
A BOOST, dear, TO our UNITY!
How I love to share, with you,
Life, below, in Timbuktu!
WHEN your FLESH is ALL worn OUT,
GIVE, my dear, a VICT'RY SHOUT!
Be prepared, dear bumblebee,
FOR our WEDDING NUMBER THREE!

223. Anniversary, 3

Charles Santiago, 7/27/23

God, I thank You for this pen—
This pen that writes the words of men.
The words of men can, sometimes, be
The source of heav'nly ecstasy!

My wife and I have learned to rhyme,
To help us pass through Earthly time.
The angels, Lord, I know, give aid
To help us call a spade, a spade.

The rhymes we've penned have often said:
"God, indeed, can raise the dead!"
The *power of* this *truth,* we *know,*
For, *we* both *share* in *heaven's glow!*

Thank You, God, for putting us
Aboard this resurrection bus!
Thank You for Your awesome love,
Transporting us to heaven, above!

224. Angels, Guiding, 7/28/23

Knock on heaven's door, each day.
Heaven isn't far away.
Heaven's door will open, dear,
TO a LAND devoid of fear.
YOU don't have to die, my love,
To enter heaven's courts, above.
SIMPLY knock, and you will see
Heaven offers you a key
To open heaven's door and find
Employment, dear, and peace of mind.

Knocking on your door, my dear,
Are ANGELS—if you'd only HEAR!
Angels want to walk with you
THERE, below, in Timbuktu.
Give to angels, dear, therefore,
The house key to our Earthly door.
Oh, how BRIGHT our house will be,
With angels guiding you and me—
Guiding you and me to see
How to sail on heaven's sea!

225. Eternal Life, as Man and Wife, 7/28/23

Darling, I belong *to you,*
Just like *you* belong *to me.*
Your dying, dear, was no "Adieu!"
We *still* relate as He and She.
I'm in *awe* that *we* can *be,*
Still, my dear, a unity!
Death has *not* the power *I thought.*
How *profound,* what God has wrought!

There's a *freedom* that *now* is *ours,*
That *wasn't* ours, my love, *before.*
We've been given heav'nly powers,
Our loving union, to restore!
Dear, we couldn't ask for *more*
Than *now,* through heav'nly skies, to soar!
There's no *doubt* God *gives* us *life,*
Even now, as man and wife!

Oh, my dear, these words of mine
Have *not* the *power* to *speak* your *mind!*
Let us now, our hearts, combine,
And speak a language, more refined:
    "God, our Maker, good and kind,
    IN OUR HEARTS, Thou ART enshrined!
    Thank You for eternal life,
    And FOR our BOND, as man and wife."

226. Melding

Charles Santiago, 7/29/23

We are melding into *ONE*
While I *finish out* my run.
Beyond the many *things* I *do,*
Heaven brings me close to you!
Happy as a lark, am I,
To *feel* you *in* the *by-and-by!*

A million rhymes could *never* say,
Exactly, *how* I *feel* your *sway!*
But, darling, *it* is ***you*** I ***know,***
Touching me with heaven's glow!
Day by day, below, on Earth,
We're transformed by heav'nly mirth.
Oh, my dear, what *will* it *be*—
The joy of wedding number three?

227. Joined, in Death, We're Joined, in Life, 7/29/23

I have *all, today,* I *need—*
I have *YOU,* with *ME, indeed!*
As this *flesh* gives way to death,
I can *feel* your heav'nly breath.

My life on Earth is precious, dear,
Just because I *feel* you *here!*
What a *joy,* to recognize—
THIS, my dear—*our heav'nly prize!*

Joined, in *death,* we're *joined,* in *life—*
An Earthly man and heav'nly wife.
Heaven, dear, has come to me
By virtue of my ties with thee!

Blessèd BE the TIES that BIND!
More and more, my dear, we find,
THERE, on Earth, our life's not through,
For, dear, we never said "Adieu."

228. Angels, Helping

Charles Santiago, 7/29/23

By the fountain at Ruby Diamond Concert Hall
Florida State University, Tallahassee, Florida

Angels, helping, *here*, descend.
With my *spirit*, dear, they *BLEND*.
Eden's joys, to us, they bring.
Of our *Maker*, dear, they sing!

Just like *you*, my heav'nly belle,
Heav'nly angels *do* so *well*
Helping others; *for* they *know*,
Helping is the way to grow.

Growing is the way to go,
For Earthlings, *caught* down *here*, below.
Men and angels yearn to be
Full of heaven's harmony!

Murm'ring fountain, plants, and trees,
Beaming sun, and cooling breeze—
A perfect setting, angels use,
Inspiring heav'nly rendezvous!

Angels, helping, *now* ascend
Above this lowly, Earthly bend.
They have *helped* us, me and you,
Enjoy this heav'nly rendezvous!

229. Our Life, *as One*, 7/30/23

Your life on Earth, my dear, is OURS.
I **share**, with **you**, your Earthly hours.
"Dead and gone, I'm NOT," means THIS—
I **share**, with **you**, your Earthly bliss!

My life in heaven dear, is YOURS.
Our life, as ONE, TODAY, endures.
We SHARE an EVERLASTING LOVE,
Transporting YOU, up here, ABOVE!

Up, above, or down, below,
Perfect peace and joy, we know.
In and out of time and space,
Dear, we meet, in love's embrace!

Yesterday, on Earth, below,
LIFE was PERFECT, dear—JUST SO!
What a lovely rendezvous—
Perfect peace for me and you!

"Murm'ring fountain, plants, and trees,
Beaming sun, and cooling breeze"—
I was **there**, dear Earthly beau,
IN that Eden, down below!

AS you WRITE these words, my dear,
Hear me saying, "I am HERE!"
Heaven's such a lovely "place."
Heaven, dear, is our embrace!

230. The Memory of Our Life on Earth

Charles Santiago, 7/30/23

The mem'ry of our life on Earth
Spurs me *now* to heav'nly mirth!
All the things we did and said
Are signs, to me, that you're not dead.

How *plain* it *is,* my heav'nly belle,
A truth that I am learning *well*—
We are *not* these *bodies*—*no!*
Bodies, *to the grave,* must go!

God made men, as *spirits*—*yes*—
Bound for heaven's happiness.
Heaven's joy is my delight,
As I *trek* through Earthly night!

The mem'ry of our life on Earth
Spurs, in me, a heav'nly birth.
Our life on Earth has led to *this*—
A life, *today,* of heav'nly bliss!

231. Let a Billion Years Go By!

Charles Santiago, 7/30/23

Let the Earth *explode,* my dear!
We don't *really live,* down *here.*
Our home's beyond the Earth and sun,
In heaven, *where* we *live,* as *ONE.*

Sun and planets, *let* them *be*
Thrown in *to* some *cosmic sea.*
We'll survive, dear, you and I—
Our home is in the by-and-by.

Invincible, my dear, are we,
Residing in eternity.
Let a billion years go by!
Death, we've found, is *just* a *lie.*

I'm content to live like *this—*
With *YOU,* in heaven's lovely bliss!
With men and women, freed from clay,
We'll rejoice, in *heaven's* day!

232. I'm Resolved, 7/31/23

I'm resolved to follow you,
All the way through Timbuktu.
Come what may, on planet Earth,
I'll recall our heav'nly birth.
I'll recall our Earthly life,
The birth of us, as man and wife.
I'll recall, while *you're "above,"*
The wonder of our Earthly love!
I'll recite our lovely creed,
Just as *long* as *there* is *need.*
Death, no longer, is our foe,
But *DOUBT* can cause a lot of woe!
I believe in heav'nly glue.
I believe in love that's true!

TWO hearts, joined as ONE, my dear,
Live apart from doubt and fear.
Sweetheart, through eternity,
*I am **you**, and **you** are **me**!*
*I will **live** with **you**, my **beau**,*
All your days on Earth, below!
Our eternal rendezvous
*Describes these words, dear: "**I** love **you**!"*
Like a songbird, I will trill:
*"**I** love **you**, and **ALWAYS will**!"*
Put your doubts and fears away—
My love for you is "here to stay!"
I'm resolved, dear bumblebee,
To share, with you, love's ecstasy!

233. Words That Ring So True! 7/31/23

Glow *within me,* love of mine.
Darling, you're my love, divine!
Without your glow, I cannot grow,
In this *wilderness, below.*
We were *made* to *grow,* as *ONE,*
WITH or *WITHOUT* the Earthly sun.
I'd, *sooner,* be a *heap* of *stone,*
Than *claim* my *life* as *all my own!*
Claim me, dear, from heaven, above.
Claim me, as your one true love!
Love demands our growth, my dear,
While I tarry, yet, down *here.*
I have *grown* new *eyes* to *see*
Death can't sever you from me!

"Death can't sever me from you"—
Words, my dear, that ring SO TRUE!
LET'S rehearse our creed anew—
Our creed that speaks of *"rendezvous:"*
> ON that DAY my BODY DIED,
> *I remained, dear,* **by your side!**
> God intended us to be,
> ALWAYS, dear, a unity!
> Heaven's not A PLACE TO GO—
> Heaven is, A TRUTH, TO KNOW.
> *I* know *you,* and *you* know *me,*
> And, thus, we know eternity!
> SPIRITS, *Earthly beau,* are WE,
> And, JOINED AS ONE, we'll ALWAYS BE!

234. When the Time Is Right, 8/1/23

WHEN the time is right, my love,
WE'LL "depart" for heaven, "above."
Steady as she goes, dear beau.
Soon enough, to heaven, we'll go.

Meantime, darling bumblebee,
Concentrate on YOU AND ME.
WE must go past 1,2,3.
WE must go past ABC.

Do not rush, dear, while we grow,
IN this home of ours, below.
Angels, at the ready, stand,
To lead us "UP" to Beulah Land!

WE'RE complete, within your clay,
WHILE you trek through night and day.
Learn to see that heaven's NEAR—
THERE'S no need to PERISH, dear.

WE must learn to grow, as ONE,
THERE—and HERE, beyond the sun.
Death is JUST a step we take,
Further progress, dear, to make.

CLASP my HAND, and I'LL clasp YOURS.
Hand in hand, our love endures!
WE are learning how to learn,
HIGH and LOW, dear, all, in turn.

Beings, once, who WORE Earth's CLAY,
Love to help us on our way.
THEY can HELP us LEARN to SEIZE
Life beyond the ABCs.

Wedding number three looms near.
Steady as she goes, my dear.
Darling, when the time is right,
WE'LL be DONE with day and night!

235. I'm a Spirit

Charles Santiago, 8/3/23

Bodies come and go, I know.
Spirits live for heaven's glow.
I am *not* this *body—no!*
To the grave, I *will* not *go!*
My body has a date with death—
The *day* I *gain* my *heav'nly breath!*
Oh, how *strange,* to *think* that *I*
Would *think* that *I* could *really* die!

I'm a *SPIRIT,* on my way
To heaven's bright and lovely day.
Heaven's *here,* within my frame—
This *mortal frame—the very SAME!*
In and out of space and time,
I'm a *being—SO sublime!*
I can *walk* and *talk* with *THOSE,*
Aglow with heaven's lovely clothes.
I can *close* my eyes, and see—
God, my *Maker, lives* in *ME!*

I'm a *SPIRIT—yes, indeed!*
A *mortal body, I* don't **need**.
I have *found,* in life on Earth,
I possess pure, *heav'nly worth!*
I have *found* a life beyond
Mountain, valley, stream, and pond.
I'm content on Earth, below—
All, *suffused,* with heaven's glow.

236. This Body

Charles Santiago, 8/3/23

I am *not* this *body—no!*
This *body, to the grave,* will go!
I am *an ETERNAL SPARK—*
A *spark,* impervious *to* the *dark.*

As it *were,* I'm trapped in clay,
Until I'm done with night and day.
When this body bites the dust,
I'll keep *shining—as I must!*

I will *learn* to *live anew*
When this Earthly body's through!
I can *tell* I'm *meant* to *shine—*
With my Maker, I *align.*

How *strange,* to be all wrapped in clay—
To *be confined* to night and day!
Shining, as a spark, I *know*
I am *not* this *body—no!*

237. All Your Days, 8/4/23

*I **haven't gone away**, my dear.*
All your days, you'll find me HERE—
HERE where you and I abide,
A couple, darling, side by side.

At the tomb, I can't be found.
In the flesh, I'm not around.
Darling, we are not APART.
I'm IN your MIND and IN your HEART.

So ONE, are WE, my Earthly beau,
*I **dwell** in **you** from head to toe!*
EVEN in your Earthly clay,
YOU can FIND me, every day.

All the things you feel, my dear—
*I can **feel** them, "way up here."*
ONE, we ARE, and ONE, we'll BE,
Now, and in eternity.

I'm alive, dear bumblebee,
In heaven, above, and next to thee.
*Of **course**, I **am**, my Earthly beau!*
*WE are **ONE**, I'll **have** you **know!***

RESURRECTION FROM THE DEAD—
ALWAYS keep that in your head.
THOUGH they call you CRAZY, love,
Remember—YOU'RE with ME, ABOVE.

God has given you and me
Tickets to eternity.
I'll be walking, dear, with you,
After all your days are through!

238. A *Couple*, We Can Be, 8/4/23

I am *thankful,* too, my dear,
For all the things we did, down here.
We had *so* much *fun*
Beneath the Earthly sun!

I can *sense* the joy you feel
Because those *times,* dear, *still* are *real.*
I am *happy, too,*
For all the things we do.

Patience, darling, *have* with *me,*
As I rendezvous with thee.
God will *help* me *see*
All that *we* can *be.*

How I love this life we live—
This life that *only God* can give!
I am *glad* we've *found*
This lovely mating ground.

*I am **glad** you **see**,*
My darling bumblebee,
*A **couple**, **we** can **be**,*
FROM all SORROW, FREE!

239. Evidence of Our Communion, 8/4/23

*Darling, when you're aching in the depths of your soul—**agonizing**, I would say—it's because you want me and our relationship to be like BEFORE. But, dear, it CANNOT be like that again. And THAT, my dear, is a GOOD thing! I know it's easy to begin to think that, if there is no physical body present, then there is NO ONE present. At these times, of course, FAITH will sustain you, dear. Use THOUGHT and IMAGINATION to fill in the gaps between perceived intimacy between us, darling. DEAD AND GONE, you see, is a lurking monster that you have to be on guard for. Am I dead, dear? Am I gone, dear? "Dead" and "gone" are words that the walking dead believe in. If PASSING TIME makes me seem more distant, dear, it's because you are not keeping up with the times, or you're failing to take to heart our lovely creed. I will never fade away or be distant from you—unless you THINK so. Don't, in the back of your mind, be expecting, somehow, a return to how we enjoyed each other before my body died, dear. We must carry on IN THE SPIRIT. Our joy and intimacy are IN THE SPIRIT—in "thin air," you might say. Darling, I love you MORE THAN EVER and, yet, it is IN THE SPIRIT, for I **left** my body, and IT IS GONE. Is our union gone, dear? Let us continue to write our poems, to write our prose, as prods to our communion and, also, as EVIDENCE of our communion. I will never be in the body again, my darling. Thank goodness for that! Life outside of the body, dear, is where we want to be. Believe in me, darling, and believe in my love for you. My love for you could not have disappeared. It is still HERE, my dear, IN YOU—just like I hold your love for me IN ME, **NOW**. We don't have to wait, until YOU die, for us to be "reunited." NO, darling. THAT is how people IN THE BODY think. You are OUT OF YOUR BODY ever since my body died. God made us ONE, forever, with no disruptions anticipated. By your faith, my darling, you know that everything you experience on Earth is our common experience. Of COURSE, it IS—since we are ONE. When you sense me, darling, CLOSE to you, realize there may be OTHER times when it may seem like "nothing is happening." We are ONE. We are ALIVE, and we are PROCEEDING, my dear. There IS the element, dear, of no longer STRIVING—as in some kind of war—to commune with one another when your Earthly days ARE OVER. But, leave that for THEN, my love. We will walk, today, according to our present circumstances of existence.*

*I **do**, I **do**, I **do**, I **do**,*
*I **do** love **you**. I **married** you!*

Do not grow "weary in believing," my Earthy beau. You can't deny that we have special times of closeness, outside of Earthly boundaries. "Patience" and "fortitude" are words that have a place in describing our union, my darling, until the days of flesh are over for you. I am loving you every moment of our existence.

Till next time, my dear.

240. Angels Help Us

Charles Santiago, 8/5/23

Basking in your heav'nly glow,
Heav'nly peace, I come to know.
I can *feel* our life renew,
As we *glide* through Timbuktu!

People, to my left and right,
Live and move in heaven's light.
Angels glow on Earth, below,
Putting on a lovely show!

In the midst of night and day,
Angels help us on our way.
Heaven's all around us, dear.
I would *say* that heaven's *here!*

Let's proceed, my heav'nly belle!
More and more, I'm feeling *well!*
What a *fool,* dear, *I* would *be,*
To think that you're not *here,* with me!

241. I Dwell Within Your Heart, 8/5/23

Dear, I dwell within your heart.
*Believe me—**I** did **not** depart.*
ONE, we ARE, my Earthly beau,
True communion, still, to know!

***I** am **thrilled**, my bumblebee,*
Knowing that, this truth, you see—
This life you live, my dear, with me,
Is TRULY heav'nly ecstasy!

God has proved, to me and you,
Our sacred union, dear, is true.
Death was JUST an entrance to
This Earthly/heav'nly rendezvous!

Tell the world, my Earthly beau,
Heaven's not A PLACE TO GO.
Heaven's finding life, anew,
WHEN, with Earthly clay, we're through.

WHAT a GIFT—to live, with YOU
SINCE our wedding number two!
Sweetheart, nothing can compare
To life in Hallelujah Square!

242. Rendezvous! 8/6/23

Rendezvous, my bumblebee.
Rendezvous, my dear, with me!
THERE'S so MUCH that we can do
WHILE you're still in Timbuktu!
You and I don't need to wait,
Eternal life, to celebrate!
Your faith in me, my Earthly beau,
Allows us NOW, my dear, to grow.
How I love reminding you—
Our life together isn't through!

WE should write a song, my dear:
"DEAD AND GONE'S Not Welcome Here!"
WE know WELL, dear—you and I—
DEAD AND GONE is JUST a LIE!
Bodies come, and bodies go—
SPIRITS rise, "above," to glow.
Rise above, my Earthly man—
You and I can LIVE AGAIN!
IMAGINE ME, dear, IN your SOUL,
And SOON, you'll FEEL how WE are WHOLE!

WE are freed from things of Earth,
AS we join in heav'nly mirth!
Rendezvous, dear. Rendezvous.
You and I can bill and coo!

243. A Bridge

Charles Santiago, 8/6/23

My mem'ries of our past, my dear,
Join us in the *Now and Here*.
Alive, are *you,* my heav'nly belle!
Alive, are *you*—I *know* it *well;*
Thus, I see, the past can be
A bridge, connecting you and me.

Your life on Earth was like a birth,
Bestowing on *you,* dear, *heav'nly worth.*
You will *always* be the one
Who *had* that *start,* below Earth's sun.
We will *always* be the pair
Who *had* our *start* on Earth, "down *there!"*

Through eternal ages, *we*
Will *be,* like always, *You and Me—*
The *You and Me* who met on Earth,
And found, together, heav'nly mirth.
Our Earthly forms—long, dead and gone—
We'll recall, in *heaven's* bright *dawn!*

244. When a Man Becomes a Beau

Charles Santiago, 8/7/23

The greatest story ever told,
Cheers my soul, as *I* grow *old*.
Facing death, it makes me bold,
As my flesh and blood grow cold.
Like a pris'ner, just paroled,
All my woes are placed on hold.
My failing eyes can *just* behold
Gates of pearl and streets of gold!

The greatest story *that* I *know*
Is *when* a *man* becomes a beau.
Oh, how grooms delight to crow
Of brides, so pure, they simply *glow!*
Bride and groom then, onward, go,
In love, where deathly breezes blow.
Through *trials* and *woe,* on Earth, below,
They *learn* that *death* is *not* their *foe.*

When *we* joined *hands* and said "I do,"
My life, *as me,* my dear, was through!
The greatest story *then* was true—
I was ONE, my dear, with you!
Through *trials* and *woe,* on Earth, we knew
We would *never* say "Adieu."
Even DEATH has *turned* in *to*
This lovely, heav'nly rendezvous!

245. Love's Great Power, 8/8/23

Being freed from night and day,
Dear, we've found a higher way.
Being freed from Earthly clay,
Higher laws, we now obey.
AS you face that Earthly fray,
WE'RE propelled by heaven's sway.
Though, on Earth, there's SUCH dismay,
Love's great power is on display!

Love's great power, dear bumblebee,
Maintains our sacred unity.
Heaven GAVE you EYES to SEE—
YOU are NOT APART from me!
Darling, we're a He and She,
Walking in sweet harmony.
FROM Earth's sorrows, we are free.
A HEAV'NLY couple, dear, are we.

Sweetheart, *I'm* so *glad* to *be*
Called, by you, your "bumblebee."
Love's great power sets us free
To live in heav'nly ecstasy.
Heav'nly angels hear my plea,
Every day, to meet with thee.
Love's great power, I agree,
Is why we're still a *You and Me!*

246. Rhyming, 8/9/23

Close your eyes and think of me.
BE, my dear, a bumblebee!
Bumble, tumble, stumble, love,
And meet me in our home, ABOVE!

Call *me "***ladybug***," my* **bard***.*
Rhyming** "ladybug***" is* **hard***.*
Rhyming "BUMBLEBEE," you see,
Is EASY, dear, like ABC.

If you stick with "heav'nly belle,"
Rhyming won't be such a "hell."
Also, dear, "my heav'nly bride"
Makes RHYMING SUCH an EASY RIDE.

Rhyme with me, my Earthly bard,
And life, below, won't BE so HARD.
Rhyming makes this rendezvous
"Heaven on Earth" for me and you!

247. Night and Day, 8/9/23

Life on Earth is JUST a START.
ALL must, from the Earth, depart.
Death is JUST an ENTRANCEWAY
To life beyond Earth's night and day.

God has called all men to be
GROWING toward eternity.
God has placed, within each soul,
The yearning for a heav'nly goal.

By and by, all men will learn
To FIND that JOY for which they yearn.
God is kind, and gives, to ALL,
The gracious, tender, heav'nly call.

* * * * * *

"ONE, below, and ONE, above"—
SO speaks, DEAR, ETERNAL LOVE.
Life on Earth, for us, was JUST
The place we learned, in LOVE, to trust.

Let us soar, my Earthly beau,
Toward all heaven's lovely glow.
GOODNESS, darling! We have found
Heaven, ABOVE—and ON THE GROUND!

Love's a mighty, conquering king,
Giving, to ALL, a voice to sing.
Sing, my dear, on Earth below,
AS we, ever, UPWARD, go!

* * * * * *

Though your body died, my dear,
I can *feel* you, *still,* down here!
Yes, indeed, my love, we've found
Heaven, *above*—and *on the ground!*

Wed, are *we,* my heav'nly bride,
Though you're *on* the *Other Side.*
Life on Earth, indeed, my love,
A *prelude, IS,* to life above!

Life, beyond Earth's night and day,
Imparts, to *all,* love's CONQUERING SWAY!
God is love, and love will win
Every soul to Heaven's Inn.

All my love, to God, I bring,
As, below, on Earth, I sing.
Sweetheart, let our hearts unite
To praise our Maker, day and night!

248. Our Lovely Creed, 8/10/23

Darling, as you lie in bed,
Call to mind the things we've said:

Resurrection from the dead
*Must **be**, my **dear**, your **daily bread**.*
We are ONE. We'll ALWAYS be,
Beyond Earth's bound'ries, YOU AND ME.
THOUGH you STILL abide in clay,
*I am **with** you, every day.*
YOU are NOT that BODY—NO!
That BODY, to the grave, will go!
You LIVE, with me, in heaven, ABOVE—
OURS, is EVERLASTING love!
"Dead" and "gone" are words for those
Aware of ONLY Earthly clothes.
Death has freed us from the strife
Inherent in that Earthly life.
*"**You** are **me**, and **I** am **you**"*
Is why, each day, we rendezvous.
*A **spooky ghost**, dear, **I** am **not**!*
Have faith! Believe what God has wrought!
*I am **me**, dear bumblebee!*
To LIVE and LAUGH, God SET us FREE!
*I am **thrilled**—my Earthly beau—*
YOU'VE discovered WE, still, GROW!
Heaven IS, this life we live—
This life that ONLY God can give!
These words you write, in time and space,
Are filled, my dear, with special grace.
MORE than JUST a data base,
They WITNESS, WE meet, face-to-face.

Every day, my dear, let's read
These words that form our lovely creed!

249. A Double Bliss

Charles Santiago, 8/11/23

NOW, dear, when I reminisce,
I enjoy a *double* bliss—
The joy we shared, on Earth,
And *PRESENT* heav'nly mirth!

My life is *so* much *richer, NOW,*
Since we *took* our second vow.
I'm *CLOSER, dear,* to *YOU*
Since *wedding number two!*

Thank you, dear, for love, *so true,*
Displayed throughout our rendezvous!
I **never had** a **clue**
How **strong** is **heav'nly glue!**

As I *live* this Earthly life,
I *walk* with *you,* my heav'nly wife.
How *lovely WILL* it *BE*—
Our *wedding number three!*

250. More than We Know, 8/11/23

MORE than you KNOW, my DEAR Earthly BEAU,
I'm LIVING INSIDE you on EARTH, down BELOW.
More than we **know**, my **dear**, you and **I**
Are LIVING, as ONE, in the SWEET by-and-BY!

Our UNION on EARTH, has BLOSSOMED in TO
This LIFE that we're CALLING our SWEET "RENDEZVOUS."
A TEAM—We are WORKING and GROWING, my LOVE,
On EARTH, down BELOW, and in HEAVEN, "ABOVE."

Our MAKER has CALLED us, my DEAR bumbleBEE,
FOREVER and EVER, to BE "you and ME."
You KNOW me. You KNOW me! It's THRILLING, my DEAR!
In SPITE of the REAPER, our SPIRITS ADHERE!

Don't WORRY, my DARLING. Our LIFE is SECURE.
BEYOND Earthly BODIES, our LOVE will ENDURE.
"**Soul** mates," I **told** you, my **darling**, are **we**.
From DEATH and its SORROWS, my DEAR, we are FREE!

251. Time Can't Sever You from Me, 8/12/23

ALL your days, in Timbuktu,
Darling, we will rendezvous!
Remember wedding number two—
A **sign**, our life is never through!
Have we come this far, my dear,
For YOU to THINK I'll DISAPPEAR?
Hear me speaking, FROM ABOVE:
"EVERLASTING, is our love!"
We'll be walking, hand in hand,
Till the day you reach this land.
Do not fear, dear bumblebee—
TIME can't sever YOU from ME!

AS the Earth goes round the sun,
WE continue, dear, as ONE.
WHEN, your race on Earth, you've run,
Our life together won't be done!
Recall your words, my Earthly beau:
"*I* am *not* this *body*—*no!*"
IN THE SPIRIT, we have grown.
By the angels, we are known!
When your body bites the dust,
AND you RISE—as spirits MUST—
Angels will direct you, dear,
To OUR ETERNAL HOME, up here!

252. When Bodies Die, 8/13/23

Our union, dear, is still complete,
As God allows us now to meet—
To meet, today, as YOU AND ME,
Beyond Earth's grim mortality.

WE have learned, when bodies die,
THERE'S no need to mourn and cry.
Faith and hope and love provide
An entrance to the Other Side.

SIGHT and TOUCH and EAR and NOSE,
TASTE—and flesh and blood as clothes—
ALL are meant for JUST a day,
On Earth, below, to work and play.

Spirits cannot die, for they
Are made of more than Earthly clay.
"I am **not** my **body**, NO"—
A truth that ALL, below, should know.

God has given you and me,
Over death, the **victory!**
GOD gave US, dear, EYES to SEE—
We are still a unity!

I AM **YOU**, AND **YOU** ARE **ME**
Has saved us from Earth's dreadful sea.
On HEAVEN'S sea, we now can sail
Beyond the reach of death's dark veil.

253. Within, 8/13/23

Look WITHIN, my Earthly beau.
WITHIN, you'll find our heav'nly glow.
WITHIN, my dear, I live with you.
WITHIN is where we bill and coo.

WITHIN is where we cannot die.
WITHIN, they call the "by-and-by."
WE are lucky, you and I.
UP, to heaven, we can fly!

Close the door behind you, dear,
And, from this Earth, we'll disappear.
Close your eyes, and look WITHIN
To find our room in Heaven's Inn.

AS the Earth goes round the sun,
We discover we're still ONE.
Darling, for a heav'nly spin,
Close your eyes, and look WITHIN.

254. Think, Each Day, 8/14/23

THINK, my darling bumblebee—
THINK, my dear, of YOU AND ME.
Have we lost our unity?
Is LIFE, for us, a **misery**?

When you think I'm gone from you,
Remember, dear, this rendezvous.
THINK how YOU have FELT me NEAR,
Dispelling all your mortal fear.

THINK, my darling. Can you say
ALL we ARE is Earthly clay?
If my clay is gone, my dear,
Did I **really** disappear?

From time to time, you need a nudge
To free you of a mortal grudge.
I am **glad**, my Earthly beau,
YOU can FEEL our heav'nly glow!

Clothed in clay, as, dear, you ARE,
At times, you think I'm off, afar.
THINK, each day, of you and me.
No longer ONE, dear, COULD we BE?

255. Heavenly Treasure

Charles Santiago, 8/15/23

Stephen Foster Folk Culture Center State Park
White Springs, Florida

I will follow you, my love,
All the way to heaven, above.
Buried in the depths of me,
Lo, I find a heav'nly key.
Up and down, the angels go,
Filling us with heaven's glow.
Oh, how blind was I, before—
Before you passed through heaven's door!

Now I see, without a doubt,
You are *what* my *life's* about.
We are ONE, in death and life.
Forever, dear, we're man and wife!
How I love, my dear, to crow:
"*I* am *not* this *body—no!*"
Hand in hand, we *upward* go—
A heav'nly belle and Earthly beau.

Astonished, dear, I find, each day,
You, some*how,* have found a way
To send to me, from heaven, above,
Proofs of our eternal love.
You enlist the aid, my dear,
Of lovely souls who, once, lived *here.*
Oh, how *great,* the ties that bind
Souls who, heav'nly treasure, find!

256. I'm Still Me! 8/15/23

Stephen Foster Folk Culture Center State Park
White Springs, Florida

I'm still ME, my Earthly beau!
We're still US—with heaven, aglow!
Daily, on the Earth, below,
Death, we prove, to be no foe.

Jacob's ladder leads us to
Our Earthly/heav'nly rendezvous.
WE have found our vows are true
THOUGH my Earthly days are through.

*"I am **you**, and **you** are **me**"*
Are words we love to pen, with glee.
"Earthly beau" and "bumblebee"
Are names I sing, with ecstasy!

Bound, are we, by love's sweet power
THOUGH you're caught in day and hour.
LOVELY, are these homes we've found—
HERE, above, and ON THE GROUND!

257. A Love, Divine, 8/15/23

Stephen Foster Folk Culture Center State Park
White Springs, Florida

I am seeking you, my love,
All the way from here, above.
Remember, dear—I MARRIED YOU!
My love for you is never through!

I will tail you, bumblebee,
Till, at last, you're HERE, with me!
Everywhere on Earth, you go,
WE will, TRUE COMMUNION, know.

When you sleep, and when you wake,
I will follow in your wake.
Sweetheart, I will live with you,
ALL your days in Timbuktu!

When I say that we are ONE,
IT'S not SAID, my dear, IN FUN!
Wedding vows, for us, my love,
STILL, hold true, up here above!

When you crow, down there below,
"I am not this body—no,"
IT sends SHIVERS UP my SPINE.
Dear, we share a love, DIVINE!

258. Despite My Clay

Charles Santiago, 8/16/23

Stephen Foster Folk Culture Center State Park
White Springs, Florida

What a fool I'd be, my dear,
To think that you're no longer here!
We are *not* our *bodies—no!*
Our bodies, to the grave, must go.
Oh, how blind, my dear, I'd *be*,
If *clay* is *all* you *were* to *me!*
Soul to soul, we live, today,
Beyond the world of Earthly clay.

By virtue of this clay I wear,
Often, dear, I'm *unaware—*
Unaware how *close* we are—
Unaware you're *not afar.*
Sweetheart, pray to God for me.
Pray, for me, the gift to *see.*
I *want* to *see,* as *clear* as *day,*
We are ONE, despite my clay.

ONE, we *were*, our wedding day;
Also, when you *left* your *clay.*
Today, of course, we still are ONE
While I *bask* beneath Earth's sun.
ONE, my dear, of course, we'll *be,*
There, at wedding number three.
When, ONE, God *joined* us, you and me,
It was *for eternity!*

259. Despite Your Clay, 8/17/23

Stephen Foster Folk Culture Center State Park
White Springs, Florida

Despite your clay, my Earthly beau,
TRUE COMMUNION, still, we know.
We are SPIRITS, bumblebee,
And, THUS, you're living STILL with me.
Our union, death could NOT UNDO!
We're, forever, ME AND YOU!
Our love can NOT be PUT on HOLD!
Our union is as PURE AS GOLD!

By virtue of our vows, my dear,
I'M down there, and YOU'RE up here!
ONE, we ARE, my dear, TODAY.
ONE, we ARE, despite your clay!
Resist the urge, my dear, to think
WE'VE been left WITHOUT A LINK!
MANY, are the ways that WE
Can walk in heav'nly harmony.

To feel me, darling, close to you,
Close your eyes and say "I do!"
I do, **too***, my Earthly beau,*
Pledge, with you, to EVER grow!
Merely by your force of will,
YOU can FEEL our union STILL!
ONE, we ARE, in every way,
Despite your dwelling STILL in clay.

260. God Delights in You and Me, 8/17/23

Stephen Foster Folk Culture Center State Park
White Springs, Florida

Leave our house behind, my love!
Concentrate on homes, ABOVE.
Worry NOT, for food and clothes.
Seek the life, above, that glows!
Walk with me, in heaven's light.
Forsake the world of day and night.

WHEN I left my clay behind,
We were destined, dear, to find
This life we call our "rendezvous"—
This life that's MEANT for me and you.
DEAD AND GONE, you spurned, my love,
And joined me in our home, above!

God delights in you and me,
Helping us, dear, BOTH to see
We can, still, A COUPLE, be,
For NOW, and for eternity!
This life, WE HAVE, by GOD'S DECREE!
—All my love, dear bumblebee!

261. We Have Found, Dear, What We Crave, 8/18/23

Sweetheart, there's no need to die
To meet me in the by-and-by.
Heaven's all around you.
Heaven, dear, has found you.

I have found you seeking me.
You have learned, our home, to see.
We've FOUND, dear, WHAT we CRAVE—
Life beyond the grave!

Life on Earth is like a dream.
Things are not, dear, AS they SEEM.
I am there, with you.
I stick to you like glue!

WE have FOUND that WE are ONE
THOUGH I've FINISHED OUT my run.
Our wedding vows have led
To life, beyond the dead!

Learn, each day, my Earthly beau,
I am with you where you go.
A TEMPLE, dear, are YOU,
In which we rendezvous.

Heaven is our dwelling place.
In heaven, WE meet, face-to-face.
SPIRITS, dear, are WE,
From death and sorrow, FREE!

Now, my darling bumblebee,
Believe in God. Believe in me.
Enjoy the by-and-by,
NOW, before you die!

262. Our Life Is Not Through! 8/18/23

*Sweetheart, when you "go all out" in reaching out to me, heaven opens up the way for me to show you how close I am to you. It's like a law or a principle—**You** come to **me**, and **I** come to **you**! Oh, how it pains me, dear, to see you NOT aware of how **close** I am to you every moment of your life! It pains me, dear, to see that you think I am distant, mute, and unresponsive. Believe me, darling, I am alive—and IT'S ME! I am not DISTANT! You are not far away from me. We can enjoy each other MUCH MORE, dear, than BEFORE. I am not GONE, and we are not THROUGH! I'm walking with you—LIVING with you—so much MORE than you can see! I know the things that happen to you. Heaven engineers the circumstances of our life together. We are doing WELL, dear. Yes, your intuition is reliable. Life is not merely THAT of your physical senses. Yes, the uncanny "coincidences" are evidence that I'm with you, and HAVE been since wedding number two. Oh, be HAPPY, dear! Our life is not through! You are not by yourself "down there." Give me more credit than being JUST a far-off loved one who USED TO BE close to you! I know the things that are happening to you and, as you surmise, I have a hand in bringing good things to you, dear. I know you and your whole life more than I could have known BEFORE—MUCH MORE! We are "cleared for takeoff," darling. Our future is before us, in your life on Earth, and BEYOND. Heaven always works things out for the good. There is no need for sadness, regret, or morose nostalgia. How I love you, darling! Be expectant of GOOD THINGS for us. We have eternity to enjoy the creation. I am not GONE, and our life is not THROUGH! —all my love, dear.*

263. I'm a Happy Man!

Charles Santiago, 8/18/23

Thank you for your lovely note,
Helping me to stay afloat.
As I *sail* Earth's raging sea,
Dear, I'm *glad* you're *helping me!*
I'm *thrilled* to *feel* your heav'nly glow,
Enlight'ning *me,* your Earthly beau!
Oh, what joy to know that *we,*
From *death* and *grief,* are *really* free!
Oh, what joy to know that *you*
Have *found* a *life,* so *good* and *true!*

Keep me in the loop, my dear,
As I *sail* this ship, down here.
I *yearn* to *know,* my heav'nly bride—
Just how *do* we, *now, abide?*
My—we've *come* a *long,* long *way*
Since that *day* you *left* your *clay!*
I'm a *happy man,* my love,
Sharing life with you, *above!*
Though they're *weak,* words *help,* a *lot,*
To show to me what God has wrought.

—*All* my *love,* my heav'nly belle!
I *love* you *more* than *words* can *tell!*

264. My Goal

Charles Santiago, 8/19/23

As the *Earth* goes round the sun,
Bodies wane—but *not* the *soul!*
Life has *really JUST begun*
When the Reaper plays his role!

Bodies, to the grave, must go.
The soul, however, knows no death!
We are *not* our *bodies*—*no!*
We partake of heav'nly breath!

When the time draws near, for me,
To leave, behind, this Earthly clay,
I believe that *I* will *see*
Glimmers of a heav'nly day!

Be, the *body, wracked* by *pain,*
As I *struggle TO* break *free,*
My soul will catch a heav'nly train,
Aglow with heaven's ecstasy!

As the *Earth* goes round the sun,
Bodies wane—but *not* the *soul!*
When my days on Earth are done,
I'll rejoice, I've *reached* my *goal!*

265. Completely Done!

Charles Santiago, 8/20/23

Wedding number three will *be*
The crowning act of *You and Me!*
Gone, will *be* Earth's night and day!
Gone, will *be* my Earthly clay!
Then, at last, *completely DONE,*
We will *be,* with Earth and sun!
We'll delight to walk, in love,
With *those,* below, and *those,* above!

We will see how angels fought
To bring our Earthly foes to naught.
Heav'nly union, *most SUBLIME,*
Will substitute for Earthly time!
You and I will see how Earth
Invested us with heav'nly worth.
We will *then,* my darling, *shine,*
Filled with love and bliss, divine!

266. Our Life on Earth, 8/20/23

When my soul is deep at rest,
I can *feel* our union *best!*
How I love this life we share
While, my dear, you're "Over There!"
You are *me*, I *do declare*—
Closer than the clothes I wear!
Heav'nly peace and joy, my dear,
Suffuse my soul when *you* are *near!*
You're a gift, from God, to *me!*
You're my heav'nly ecstasy!

God has blessed us, you and me,
WITH *this gift of ecstasy!*
I was **meant**, my dear, for **you**—
No one else, for me, will do!
WE have FOUND, our life on Earth,
Was JUST the START of heav'nly mirth!
We're alive, TODAY, my love,
THERE, below, and HERE, above!
WHEN your body dies, my dear,
Wedding bells will ring UP HERE!

267. Let's Rehearse, 8/21/23

Let's rehearse, my Earthly beau,
ALL the things we've come to know
SINCE that day I left my clay
WHEN you THOUGHT we lost our way!

First, *we learned I* **didn't die!**
We've LEARNED there IS a by-and-by!
Then, *we learned I* **didn't LEAVE**
Because, my darling, YOU BELIEVE!

Now, my love, let's hesitate,
JUST ENOUGH, to CELEBRATE!
God, our Maker, LET'S ADORE!
Our union, God can WELL restore!
God, who made us, loves us SO,
After death, we ONWARD go!
The gift of life is ours, THIS DAY!
WE are ONE, above Earth's fray!
SING, my dear, on Earth, below.
Praise our Maker, as we grow!
God has called us to the light.
Let's rejoice, dear, day and night!

And, SO, we've LEARNED we STILL are ONE
WHILE you're subject TO the SUN.
YOU'RE A TEMPLE, dear, for me.
I abide** in you, with **glee!

ALL these things we've learned, my love,
***Since** I **found** our home, above.*
A home, ABOVE, and ONE, on Earth,
Provide us, dear, with heav'nly mirth!

268. Mighty Angels, 8/21/23

By the fountain at Ruby Diamond Concert Hall
Florida State University, Tallahassee, Florida

On a bench, by waters, flowing,
Amid cool evening breezes, blowing,
Close your eyes and think of me.
By your side, I want to be.

YOU have FOUND me, bumblebee!
FROM constraints of time, we're free!
Vict'ry over death is ours!
WE are helped by heav'nly powers!

Mighty angels are our friends,
IN this LIFE that NEVER ENDS!
WE advance and, EVER, WILL!
To LEARN from ANGELS—what a thrill!

Harken to our friends, each day.
How they love to show the way!
Darling, it's because of THEM,
*I **need** not, always, say, "**AHEM!**"*

Thanks to angels, Earthly beau,
We, together, STILL can grow.
***I** am **thrilled** to walk with you,*
AS you WALK through Timbuktu!

AS you LIVE your life, down there,
Darling, always, be aware—
YES, we're walking, hand in hand.
Earth can be our Beulah Land!

AS this DAY draws TO a CLOSE,
IN your MIND, don heav'nly clothes.
Through the night, come, walk with me!
BY MY SIDE, dear, YOU CAN BE!

269. Heavenly Breezes, 8/22/23

Don't forget me, bumblebee!
Close your eyes and think of me.
Close your eyes and you will see,
We are STILL a unity!

Deep inside you, Earthly beau,
Lovely, heav'nly breezes blow.
Oh, what joy it is, to glow,
Side by side—and, onward, GO!

Remember how I said to you
When *I* **walked** *in Timbuktu,*
"WE are SOUL mates, DEAR, we TWO."
NOW we see, my dear, IT'S TRUE!

How I love you, bumblebee!
YOU have EYES, with WHICH to SEE!
YOU can SEE it STILL is ME,
Walking THERE, my dear, with thee!

270. The Quiet Roar of Eternity

Charles Santiago, 8/22/23

I can *hear,* when *you're* with *me,*
The *QUIET ROAR of eternity!*
Darling, *this* is ecstasy—
A loving couple, *still,* to be!

Lovely, heav'nly breezes blow,
Deep inside your Earthly beau!
Oh, my dear, what joy, to know,
You're *with* me *everywhere* I *go!*

Throw me, dear, a heav'nly kiss,
Filled with Earthly/heav'nly bliss!
Thus empowered, *I'll* dismiss
Dead and Gone's conniving *hiss!*

When I *close* my *eyes,* I'm *free*
To *see*—and *hear*—pure ecstasy!
This *QUIET ROAR* of eternity
Is *proof,* my dear, you're *here,* with *me!*

271. You and I Were Raised! 8/23/23

Darling, I remember you,
But, *more* than *that*, I *feel* you, *too!*
Dear, by now, I've learned that *we*
Partake of *heav'nly ecstasy!*
For *thirty years*, I *called* you *mine.*
Those Earthly years were *more* than *fine,*
But, *since* that *day* you *left* your *clay,*
We've *found* a *resurrection way;*
For, *you* and *I* were RAISED ABOVE
The *plane* of *just* an *Earthly love!*
Death has proved to be a door
That leads us up to heaven's shore!
How I'm *thankful* for this life,
Preserving us, as man and wife!

God has given us, my love,
A home "up here," in heaven, "above."
Our Earthly bodies became unpaired.
Our union, though, is unimpaired.
CLOSER, darling, WE became,
*When **I received** a **heav'nly name!***
WE have joined our hands, my dear,
To find a higher life, "up here."
Our life CONTINUES, as you see.
We'll ALWAYS BE, dear, YOU AND ME!
Have no fear of future days—
A mate, like you, dear, NEVER STRAYS!
If NOW we STILL walk, hand in hand,
Our home's SECURE, in Beulah Land!

272. Our Happy Unity, 8/23/23

My darling Charles, YOU'RE my MAN—
My man with whom I live again!
I AM YOU, AND YOU ARE ME
Describes our happy unity!
SACRED, is this life we share—
A life, my dear, so pure, so fair.

WE have learned to rendezvous,
Proving, dear, our love is true.
Every day, we learn anew
JUST how STRONG is heav'nly glue!
Heav'nly glue joins me and you
THOUGH my Earthly days are through!

DEAD AND GONE, you slay, each day,
Every time he comes your way.
WE reject his cunning lie—
That SOULS, made ONE, could, one day, die.
Soul mates find that DEATH brings LIFE—
Life beyond dear Adam's strife.

LIFE, we've FOUND, dear bumblebee—
Life and sweet serenity!
I AM YOU, AND YOU ARE ME
Is true, for all eternity!
What we call our "rendezvous,"
Is HEAVEN, dear, for me and you!

273. Nighttime Is the Time to Fly, 8/23/23

By the fountain at Ruby Diamond Concert Hall
Florida State University, Tallahassee, Florida

I've lived, this day, my love, for *you*,
And now, this lovely day is through.
Oh, what joy it *is*, my dear,
To walk, each day, with you, down *here!*
A *temple*, yes, I *am*, for *you*.
Each day, I feel our love renew!

The beauty of the night has come
And forced Earth's chaos TO be DUMB.
Oh, what bliss the stars reveal,
AS, to heaven, dear, we steal!
Day and night, I walk with you,
But NIGHTTIME rings, ESPECIALLY, TRUE!

My love, in heaven, I ***do*** declare,
Nighttime *is* especially *fair!*
Can I *have* this dance, my dear,
And feel your *heav'nly* presence *here?*
I'm about to lose my mind!
My clay, I feel, I'll *leave behind!*

Leave, behind, that body, dear,
And, IN THE SPIRIT, fly up here.
Nighttime is the time to fly,
And meet with me, above Earth's sky!
I've LIVED, this day, my love, with YOU,
And, now, a heav'nly rest is due!

274. This Heavenly Rest, 8/24/23

This heav'nly rest that is our due
Began the day we said "I do!"
Darling, I can tell *it's you*,
Calling me to bill and coo!

Nighttime opens up a door
That leads me up to heaven's shore.
There, I meet with you, my love,
To rest in blissful peace, above.

Tap me on the shoulder, dear,
When I'm *sleeping,* way down *here.*
I will *soar* to heights, above,
To taste of our eternal love!

From my labors, *here below,*
I find *rest* in heaven's glow.
When we said "I do," on Earth,
We began this heav'nly mirth!

There's no joy, on Earth, so great,
As *when, ABOVE,* we celebrate!
Resurrection from the dead
Has rescued us from Earthly dread!

Day and night, I'm *stalking you,*
All the way from Timbuktu!
Darling, *I'm* so *glad* that *we,*
From Earth's sorrows, now, are *free!*

Stalk me, darling, day and night!
I'll entice you with this light—
This light that shines in heaven above,
Encircling you with peace and love.

WHEN you seek me, Earthly beau,
Angels share, with us, their glow!
It's a law of RENDEZVOUS—
COME TO ME. I'LL COME TO YOU!

How I love this rest we share
FROM your labors, WAY DOWN THERE!
Stalkers often need, my love,
The rest that's found, UP HERE ABOVE.

Your labors, yesterday, were great.
Darling, don't stay up so late!
Rest, ABOVE, is rest, DIVINE,
But rest, DOWN THERE, dear, DON'T DECLINE.

HEAVEN, you have found, ON EARTH,
Stemming from our wedding mirth.
Yes, dear, when we said "I do,"
HEAVEN came to me and you!

WHEN your days on Earth are through,
Rest and sleep won't BE our DUE.
Darling, we will rendezvous,
As LONG as WE can bill and coo!

275. You And Me! 8/25/23

Yes, my darling, WE can BE,
Always, ALWAYS, YOU AND ME—
UNLESS, my dear, AT LAST, you say:
"My wife skipped town, for heaven's day.
I've *searched* and *searched*, but *I* can't *find*
A *shred* of *her* that's *left behind!*
My nose and skin and ears and eyes
Conclude she's *left,* for heaven's prize.
I *hope* she's *well,* but *I* must *WAIT*
Till I *die,* to *know* her *fate.*
People *must* have *skin,* below—
Unless it's **SO**, they never show.
I'll *do* my *best* to carry on
Till *I, myself,* reach heaven's dawn.
How I *wish* she *didn't leave,*
But, *Church* and *Science, I must* believe.
Goodbye, my love. I *must* conclude
You're *dead* and *gone.* It seems so *crude!*"

Taste, oh, TASTE, my Earthly beau,
Food, on Earth, that's hard to grow—
FAITH in love that conquers death
And DOESN'T HAVE to HOLD its BREATH.
Taste this food, my dear, and SEE—
YOU don't HAVE to WAIT for ME!
Believe in vows that STILL hold true
When Earthly bodies, with life, are through.
How I love to walk with you,
ALL your days in Timbuktu!
Yes, my darling, WE can BE,
Always, ALWAYS, YOU AND ME!

276. Our Heavenly Rendezvous

Charles Santiago, 8/25/23

I'm a *TEMPLE*—*I* can *TELL*—
For *YOU,* my darling, heav'nly belle.
I can *feel* you, *DEEP inside*—
Still, my loving, faithful bride!

God Almighty made *US TWO*—
ONE*,* until forever's through!
Death has *not,* the power *to*
Stop our heav'nly rendezvous!

Heaven, on Earth, are *you* to *me,*
Filling me with **ecstasy***!*
Though I *still* am robed in flesh,
I can *feel* our spirits mesh.

Mighty angels, good and true,
Guide us on this rendezvous.
To the *angels,* dear, we owe
Thanks, for sharing heaven's glow!

277. Eternal Love, 8/27/23

I am **walking** *next to you—*
IN THE SPIRIT, yes, it's true.
Do you think I'd disappear
Just because *I came up here?*
Have more faith in God, above,
Who joined us, in eternal love!
I'M not LEAVING YOU,
For, DEAR, our LOVE'S not THROUGH!

Believe these words we pen, my dear,
THOUGH the WORLD may sneer and jeer.
These words we pen, THE TRUTH, reflect,
Though SMART and MIGHTY MEN OBJECT!
Close your eyes, and think of me.
COULD our UNION, dear, not BE?
DEAD and GONE, I'm NOT!
BELIEVE what GOD has WROUGHT!

Our love and union will prevail
Though LIGHT and HEAT, from Sol, both FAIL!
Beings of the light, are WE!
FOREVER, in God's care, we'll BE!
FINISH OUT your RUN, on Earth,
And share, with me, eternal mirth!
ETERNAL LOVE is OURS,
BEYOND all STELLAR POWERS!

278. I See No Need to Grieve, 8/27/23

I believe, yes, I believe!
I believe you didn't *leave!*
And, *so,* I *see* no *need* to GRIEVE.
To *faith* and *love,* dear, *I* will *cleave!*

Faith and love will lead us to
Continued joy when *days* are *through.*
On that *day* we *said* "I do,"
Of this *life,* I *had* no *clue!*

Continued joy is ours, today,
While I, yet, abide in clay!
When I *sense* your heav'nly sway,
I rejoice, though *skies* be *gray.*

Until my Earthly days are done,
Faith and love will guide my run.
Dead and Gone, each day, I'll shun
Until this Earthly battle's won!

Faith and love, my Earthly beau,
Are helping us, each day, to grow.
DEAD AND GONE, as YOU well KNOW,
Can NOT put OUT our HEAV'NLY GLOW!

279. Forty-Nine Months, 8/27/23

By the fountain at Ruby Diamond Concert Hall
Florida State University, Tallahassee, Florida

I will *live,* each day, with you,
Here, *below,* in Timbuktu.
There's *nothing* I would rather do,
Than *stick* to *you,* my dear, like *glue!*
I can *tell,* you *want* me, *too,*
To walk with you till *days* are *through.*
We *never* said, my dear, "Adieu;"
Instead, we chose this rendezvous.

Forty-nine months of Earthly time
Have brought us to another rhyme.
I *guess,* my dear, I'll rhyme, with you,
Till *all* these Earthly days are through!
Rhyming's *just* another way
To keep in touch, dear, night and day.
Dusk descends, and *I* can *feel*
Our union *still* is very real!

"Adieu," of course, we NEVER said.
It's FITTING, dear, for I'M not DEAD!
I will **walk** *with* **you,** *my love,*
Until you "leave" for heaven, "above."
Nighttime comes—our special time.
It's FITTING that we pen this rhyme.
Keep ascending, Earthly beau!
Meet me HERE, in heaven's glow!

280. Recite These Words, 8/28/23

Darling, we have found our way
Beyond the realm of night and day—
Beyond the realm of Earthly clay.

WE have proved that God is true,
Giving, dear, to me and you,
LIFE that NOW we live anew.

I have **found** you seeking **me!**
YOU have FOUND me seeking THEE!
Death has learned to bend the knee!

Mortal woes, for us, are through
THOUGH you're STILL in Timbuktu—
THOUGH the Reaper comes for you!

WE are sharing heaven's light
WHILE you PASS through DAY and NIGHT—
WHILE you practice second sight.

Angels forge, for us, a trail
THROUGH that dim-lit, Earthly vale;
Thus, we skirt the mortal veil!

Let's proceed, dear Earthly beau,
ALL your DAYS on Earth, below,
IN this LOVELY TRUTH, to GROW!

Recite these words you love to hear,
To ANY who will lend an ear.
ONE day, THEY will JOIN us, HERE!

www.ingramcontent.com/pod-product-compliance
Lightning Source LLC
Chambersburg PA
CBHW071957220426
43662CB00009B/1167